LOVE IS KING

B. B. KING'S DAUGHTER FIGHTS TO PRESERVE HER FATHER'S LEGACY

SHIRLEY KING
AND DAVE SMITHERMAN

Published in the USA by:
BearManor Media
P O Box 71426
Albany, Georgia 31708
www.bearmanormedia.com

ISBN: 978-1-62933-155-3
BearManor Media, Albany, Georgia
Printed in the United States of America
Book design by Robbie Adkins, www.adkinsconsult.com
Cover photo: Caption: John "Nunu" Zomot

TABLE OF CONTENTS

DEDICATION
To my daddy

Acknowledgements

In writing this book, I have been assisted by Dave Smitherman, Phil and Lora Stark, and my agent, Diane Nine. Thanks to their hard work for making this happen.

I especially want to thank my father, who I love with all my heart and soul. He gave me the raw talent while I was growing up and left me with all the respect and love that he gave so freely to everybody he met in the world.

Thank you to my family: my kids Venus Bryant and Patrick Johnson; my grandkids Tashawn Carter and Jasmine Johnson; and the guy who has hung in there with me for eleven years, Mr. Gerald Noel.

Thank you to one of my best friends, who has been assisting me during some dark times, Miss Gerri Wilson and her family.

I would also like to acknowledge my mother, Mary Elizabeth Gilmer, and my brother, Curtis Lee Gilmer, and his better half, Laberta. They are taking care of my mother, who is suffering from the same disease my father had.

As a result of this project, I've been able to reconnect with my mother's side of the family and learn more about them and their many musical talents.

Thanks to everyone who took time out to say something nice about me or my father for this book. I'd also like to acknowledge those who gave me a chance to work in this business and for that I will always be grateful.

Finally, thanks to Mr. Jay B. Ross, a Chicago lawyer, who gave me the name "Daughter of the Blues" some twenty years ago.

It's my hope that through sharing my story, everyone will better understand what it's like to be Shirley King, "Daughter of the Blues" and daughter of the legendary B. B. King.

Chapter 1 - The Blues Juice Blues

On Wednesday, September 16, 2015, Mr. Riley B. King would have been ninety years old. Unfortunately he passed just a few months back on May 14, 2015. That's why I was sitting at a half-moon-shaped booth right in front of the stage at this Blues bar. This New Orleans-style nightclub was tucked back off the main drag of Nashville, down a narrow cobblestone street that opens up to an area called Printer's Alley. The bar was a throwback to the old-school nightclubs, just like the ones my daddy started off in back in the 1950s. He became a legend not just for his music but also for his non-stop touring. The world had never seen a performer so dedicated to the road, and probably never will again. So, it seemed fitting that I was performing there that night, all the way from my home in Chicago, to pay tribute.

It wasn't the easiest night for me since this was the first time my father wasn't around on his birthday. I was still trying to process that, but if he taught me one thing, it was that the show must go on . . . always. That's the way my daddy, who was, of course, better known as B. B. King, always lived his life.

"Can I get you a drink?"

I turned to see a pretty dark-haired waitress smiling at me.

"Hmm, I do need a drink, especially tonight. What's good?" I asked.

This young thing looked at me for a minute like she was really giving it some thought. "How about the Blues Juice? It's yummy. House special. And you are the Daughter of the Blues, after all!"

"You got a point there, honey. Well, just so it's not too strong. I got to go on stage tonight. I don't even know what's in a Blues Juice."

"Oh, no, don't worry. I'll tell them to hold back on the pour," she promised.

She took the drink orders from the others at the table, my long-time friends Phil and Lora Stark, and a friend of theirs, who had joined us. I'd known Phil and Lora for probably twenty years or so, and they were always so good to me. When I met her, we just clicked, and with her hubby Phil being in the music licensing, booking and promotion business, we all had common interests. We've had many adventures together, and I thought tonight would be another one to add to that list.

I was still waiting for my blue "whatever" drink. Now that I ordered one, I hoped it would help get me in a party mood. Usually that was no problem for me. I had been doing that for a long time, but I guess because of the circumstances and all, it was a little bit tougher that night. The more I thought about what day it was, the more my mind started to wander. Then, I realized that I needed to focus. I needed to pay attention.

As the club filled up, I started getting more and more taps on my shoulder.

"Are you Shirley?"

"Are you the one singing tonight?"

"I'm sure sorry to hear about your daddy."

Everyone was being so nice and genuine that it almost messed me up. It wasn't so easy to stay focused with all the things I was thinking about, the memories, the times on stage with Daddy, the fancy places we went to, and later the ugliness that started creeping in. No, I wasn't thinking about any of that. *Let me just sign these CDs and smile at these nice folks. They came out in the middle of the week to show their respect and have a good time.*

"Shirley, can I talk to you?" I looked over and saw a sharp-dressed man in a fedora and pin-striped suit. He tipped his hat and flashed that lead singer smile of his.

"Oh, hey! How are you? Haven't seen you in a while!"

The singer and his band had been playing in that area for years. They were a staple in the club and they had fans all over the world, thanks to their relentless touring. They always talked about "blue-eyed soul," and I didn't know much about that, but I knew this White man sure did love playing the Blues, and it showed in his performance. Anyone who knew me knew that I wouldn't say that if it wasn't true. Not to mention that he had an awesome band. I mean they were tight, and I loved how they let me sit in on one of their gigs. Not every musician was as welcoming and as giving as him. He did not hesitate to let folks get up onstage as part of his show. Of course, they had to bring the talent or he would find a way to ease them right back into my seat. If they could do that, if they could entertain the audience and keep up with the band, he was always ready for some craziness, and that's just what I needed tonight.

"I'm good, Shirley," he said, beaming. "You look great! I was thinking I'd bring you up in the middle of the first set and you can do a couple of songs. Then, after the break, you can come back up for a couple more. You good with that?"

"Oh, you know I am and that sounds perfect," I said, smiling at him.

"What songs are you thinking about doing?"

See, that's the guy I knew. He had always been a hustler, a born entertainer. I met him over thirty years ago, when he brought me to perform in one of his shows in Cincinnati. I tried to pay him back by inviting him to Chicago for a show with me and maybe my dad, but it just did not work out. At the time, I didn't really understand the business side of things, but I was learning. I think Daddy was afraid people were using me to get to him, and maybe sometimes they were, but if someone was as good as this man, I thought it was worth a try.

I'm sure he was disappointed and probably a little offended by it, but that didn't slow him down. He was eventually the opening act for my father, and he created his own opportunity. They played maybe fifteen shows together, even three nights at the B. B. King Blues Club in Times Square! I know they talked for hours after they performed. That just shows how two professional musicians can come together for the music. Daddy was being protective of me, like he always was. I know he loved talking about the Blues with B.B. He always told me Daddy was "a class act."

Daddy never wanted me to ride on his coattails. He felt if I was performing, it shouldn't be because I was trying to be like him. He wanted to make sure it was something I wanted to do. At first I didn't understand that, but when I realized how important it was to *earn* the King name while Daddy was alive. It made me appreciate it even more. He said, "Well, one day if I'm not around and you've made a name off of being my daughter, you might not stand as well." That was the lesson he was trying to teach me. I needed to do it on my own.

"Shirley, what songs?" the singer repeated.

Oh yes, the songs! "It's my night to do a tribute to Daddy so I'd like to do 'Let the Good Times Roll.'" I know that's a traditional Blues tune that most good bands can play with no problem. "Then, how about 'Rock Me Baby'?"

"Okay," he smiled, "my boys can handle that. Second set?"

"Hmm, of course I should do 'The Thrill Is Gone' because that's what folks want to hear. Then maybe 'Last Two Dollars.'"

"Sounds good," he said. "See you on stage!"

With that, he was gone. He had work to do and it was time for me to put everything out of my mind and sing. I think a lot of folks didn't realize what it took to do that, especially on an emotional night like this one. It was my job to make sure the audience had a good time. They didn't need to know what I'd been going through. They didn't need to know that just getting this gig was a damn struggle.

Phil initially brought up the idea of having me come to Nashville for a tribute to my dad, plus he wanted his friend to see me perform. I was fine with that, so first Phil tried booking me at the B. B. King Blues Club on 2nd Avenue, because that's a natural fit. Well, I don't know exactly what all happened, but Phil said they kept giving him the runaround without committing. I told him not to worry about that. If they don't want to book me, let's go somewhere else. I've dealt with these challenges all through my singing career. That wasn't going to slow me down one bit. Phil got in touch with this club that I was sitting in. This band performed there regularly and since we got history, he agreed that a tribute would be fun. Phil made it work like he always does, but it was a lot of back and forth. I was getting a little frustrated and almost said just forget it, but the show must go on.

As I was watching them work the crowd, my mood got a little better. Seeing them interact and perform some amazing solos, I knew those guys could handle what I wanted to do.

Soon, I saw him waving me up on stage. "We have a special guest tonight . . . ."

It was time for me to do my thing. I pulled on my sequined jacket and quickly finished up that blue-colored drink, which was definitely growing on me, by the way!

For the first set, I knew I needed to get the audience going and get them on my side. It was all about winning them over and showing them a good time. So, I was up there, sequins shining bright, and I felt much better. I sang a line and then dropped my hand for emphasis. The band followed right along, punctuating each of my gestures and then waiting for me to start again. I decided to do my thing and play with them a little before I jumped into the song. It was almost silent as the audience waited for what was next.

I practically whispered, "Are we ready to party?" There was whooping and hollering from the crowd. Woo! So, I jumped into the song and the band was right there as we kicked off "Let the Good Times Roll." The crowd started clapping along and getting into it. "Come on, everybody!" This just got me going even more, making me realize that the important thing was that I was there and up on stage. I pointed up to the balcony. "Put your hands together!" Those folks loved it and seemed to be having a great time.

Dad sometimes opened his shows with that song, so it made sense for me to do the same thing that night. Once I got the ball rolling and the audience caught up, we would all be having fun. If no one had been paying attention tonight of all nights, that would have gotten to me. My philosophy was that you shouldn't go to a show and just sit like you're listening to a CD. I mean, I guess you can, but why do you want to do that? You should feel like you're at a live show. After I'm introduced, I always re-introduce myself. I like to shoot the energy out there so people can't help but have a good time. I'm going to talk to you, I'm going to get sassy with you, and I'm going to make sure you have fun.

Usually, people think I'm going to just go from one song to another, but that's not what I did. Those folks came out after a day of work and it was my job to make sure they were entertained. I always said that if you are a performer and people aren't responding, that means you haven't done your job very well.

You know what I really loved? I just loved seeing those people—all kinds of folk from all walks of life—who I had never met before come on that musical journey with me. I loved to watch them get hyped up and accept me as an entertainer with my own style. Of course I did learn from the best. I didn't play an instrument like Lucille, the way Daddy did, but I could shake a mean hip. I even played up my age and told those folks that I could still move, it just might be a little slower. It wasn't like back when I was dancing and they called me "Shirley King the Body Queen." Still, I always tried to be eye-catching, which I learned from my father. "You have to get their attention," he said. Daddy also always told me to "make sure you look like a million dollars even if you only have one in the bank!"

Oh my goodness, that was a fun set! People were cheering and screaming as I made my way off-stage. The handsome horn player held my arm and guided me down the steps on the side of the stage. I did love a Southern gentleman, that was for sure. With this reaction from the crowd and all of the applause, I felt much better. The booking mix-up, the emotions of this night, and getting to Nashville all seemed worth it.

My friends at the table welcomed me back with open arms. People started coming up to me right and left to telling me they enjoyed the performance. I signed some autographs and then Lora tapped me on the shoulder.

"Let's go to the bathroom during the break."

So, I slid out of the booth, and we made our way to the back of the bar. As we waited in line, a woman came up to me crying.

"I was so touched by your performance. I lost my father, too. It must be so hard for you, especially tonight."

I felt so bad for her, but I saw that this seemed to be helping her, and I think it helped me a little bit. I didn't realize how tough that night was going to be. I was so focused on the gig that I didn't think a lot about how much I would be missing Daddy.

We got back to our booth as the second set started. Phil was there laughing and talking with his new friend. Ted? Mike? I didn't really catch his name since he was all the way on the other side, but they seemed happy and that's all that mattered tonight. Actually, as I looked around, everyone in the damn place was in a good mood. That wasn't always the case, I can promise that. Some audiences were tough. They wanted me to earn their attention. I tried to do that every time I got on stage, but something seemed different that night. Sort of magical. Maybe it was Daddy's spirit or maybe it was those damn blue drinks because that waitress had set another one in front of me. I'm not going to lie, it was tasty as can be.

"We're gonna bring Miss Shirley King back up on stage for you!"

He was smiling and waving me up as his band kicked into gear. The second set snuck right up on me, but I was gonna handle the stage right now. Once I was up there, I looked out at the nice folks. They were clapping and cheering once again, and that never failed to make everything better. That was when I felt so at home and truly loved. It was so overwhelming I almost thought I was going to cry, but I didn't have time for that.

"Y'all know it's a special night for me! It would have been Daddy's birthday! The amazing B. B. King would have been ninety years old!"

I stood back from the microphone as the crowd cheered for my daddy. That energy just felt so good as it washed over me. Then, I slipped off my jacket as a nod to Daddy and the way he always wore one of his favorite jackets on stage.

"Give it up for the band," I said into the mic, as the guitar player strummed along. "Give it up for this hard working group." They punctuated each sentence with a few more chords. "I hear you." Then, I started the first few notes of "The Thrill Is Gone," and the crowd loved it. I eased into it slowly, doing it my way, and I heard the horns back me up at just the right time. I was where I love to be. Maybe I loved it a little too much.

After that first set, I was feeling real good and I had started to let myself relax. Then, I was all in it. I could feel the alcohol working its sweet magic. Believe me, I usually didn't drink much during a show. I liked being in control—no, I *needed* to be in control to work with my audience—but child, by that second set, I was just turned up! Missing my dad had caused me to totally let go. I was feeling no pain. When I looked around at everything that was happening, I realized that right then I was truly happy. I felt that my dad would have been so proud.

After I gauged the audience, I could tell they wanted to have some fun, and thanks to that magic juice I'd been drinking, I was ready, too. I stopped the band by holding my hand up in the air.

"Wait, wait, wait. Everyone, please hold up a minute." I pointed to the handsome dreadlocked drummer behind me. "I'm gonna need you to follow me. Can you do that?" He nodded. "No, baby, I mean *follow* me. Can you follow the bouncing balls? Look at these right here," as I pointed to my curvy backside. "All you gotta do is follow the right one, then the left one, like this." I shook them back and forth, he pounded his drums, and the crowd started cheering.

"Ain't he cute, y'all?" I said into the mic as I finished up the song, winding it down nice and easy. I remembered that a young man in the front row asked me to dedicate that song to his girlfriend. Oops, I needed to fix that.

"Now that song was for my man over here who wanted to dedicate that to his lady, but I got to thinking, if you was my man, 'The Thrill Is Gone' wouldn't be my first choice. It's a great song for sure, don't get me wrong, but I think your lady needs to hear something a little different." The audience was clapping and cheering, not sure what I was going to do. To tell you the truth, I was figuring it out as I went along.

"You still in love with her?" I asked.

He nodded.

"Of course you are, so I got one for you."

The singer gave me that look like, *What are you doing now?* I think the whole band was thrown off a little, but pros like them don't need much to pull it back in real quick. I knew that he liked playing Rhythm and Blues (R&B) songs, so I figured this one wouldn't be too tough for them.

I started singing without music and they jumped in once they recognized the first few notes of "Let's Stay Together." The horn section picked it right up. They were so good, and for me, if the horns and bass player were with me, it all worked out. I was always in sync with the bass, maybe because I've dated a bunch of bass players, I don't know, but if that bass was right, I knew it was gonna be a good set.

I came from the old school, where women who performed worked a lot with the audience by getting them to interact. That's how I created my act, by watching to see what worked and what didn't. Sometimes, folks in an audience even talked back to me, and I welcome that.

With a mic in my hand, I said, "Come on with it."

I was supposed to stir them up, give them a laugh or two. My act pulled the audience into my world for just a little while, and then I could do whatever I wanted to do. I could get away with all kinds of things.

I used to have a chair act, where someone would come up and I would do a bit. Ladies would ask me to bring their man on stage. They knew it was part of my act. I would sing and flirt with them, maybe embarrass them a little. Later, I talked and played around and made it my own type of cabaret. I can tell you every age group responded. I had a way of not offending people. I got more reaction later because people were not used to seeing that kind of show anymore. It wasn't as common as it was back in the day.

Normally, I came off-stage and went around working the tables during the show, especially if the club was arranged the right way. That bar was more of a spectator setup with the booths and the balcony and all, so walking around was a little bit harder. I was going to just work from the stage. I was going to talk a little fun stuff and do my thing.

As I was singing "Let's Stay Together," my mind began to wander again. That melancholy song and that alcohol got me thinking about all kinds of things, such as the stuff that was going on with my dad that continued up to 2016. A little over a year before, the people that worked with my father started keeping me away from him. He lived in Las Vegas, and in April of 2014, there was a horrible review about a show Daddy had done. It was obvious that something was wrong. Since they had no choice, they allowed him to stop performing for a couple of months. They knew he was sick, but he was still selling out shows and making so much money.

Damn! I was doing it again. That song and that birthday had me so emotional. I think it helped with the song, but that sure wasn't the plan. Sometimes, the music just carried me away. I just started thinking of all the things going on in my life. It was like I was outside my body and watching myself perform, almost like I was coaching myself to move one way, or say something to the audience. Maybe that was Daddy working his magic on me.

At that moment, I realized that right there on stage was where I felt love, and maybe, like Daddy, that was my problem. For most of my life, it had been the only place I felt loved and special. I hadn't found the right man in my life, and Lord knows I tried. For the most part, I'd dated musicians, artists, what have you. I guess that made sense because I dated the people I interacted with the most, right?

Maybe I chose that song because of my history with Al Green. When he was starting out, he was playing a club in Chicago and they didn't pay him after his gig. The Master of Ceremonies of that show was a friend of mine and said, "Come meet my friend, Al Green." I didn't know who he was, but Paul had gotten me into dancing, so I trusted him. I could tell Al was a genuine man, so I told him he could sleep on my couch if he behaved himself.

He agreed and stuck to his word. (Later, I'll get into more detail about us since we ended up together for five or six years.) I also dated other famous folks like Teddy Pendergrass and Jackie Wilson, but I don't know . . . nothing ever worked out for me. Sure, I had fun and all that, yet the only thing I've always wanted is someone to spend my life with, and I was starting to get worried that it wouldn't ever happen for me. Even that night, my boyfriend came there with me, but we had been fighting like crazy. I didn't know if it was the stress of the show or what. I did know that love didn't seem to be in my future and that had me scared.

When I really look at my life as a woman in her sixties traveling and performing on stage, it makes me wonder how things turned out that way. My two kids didn't hardly come around and I never got to see my grandbaby anymore. I sure didn't want to die lonely, never feeling like I was fulfilled by the love of another person. It was almost like I'd followed my father's path a little too much. Maybe I wasn't realizing it at the time when I made those choices that I made, I don't know, to be honest. Look at me now—I was up there on stage, singing and having a good time, the life of the party, but then I was going home alone.

That was my daddy's life exactly. My kids were grown, but I wasn't close to them. I hadn't found a love that I'd always wanted, and the only place I felt really at peace was on stage. *How did I get to that place in my life?* That's what I was trying to figure out. *Did I purposely follow my father so closely that I was going to end up like him? Did my love of performing mean I couldn't love in real life?*

I looked over to my table and Phil's friend Ted-Mike-Something was smiling at me. That was my cue. "You over there! Do you love me?" He slipped his hand under his shirt and lifted it up and down like a heartbeat.

"I knew you did," I said to him, as he smiled.

Well, it was time for me to finish up that song. That man and his woman looked all kinds of happy, and that made me feel good again. Hell, that was my life story, up and down, good and bad. A lot of people asked me what it was like to be B. B. King's daughter. I told everyone the same thing: it wasn't what you might think. There was a good side and a bad side, good qualities, and negative ones.

My dad didn't talk much about us to reporters because he didn't want to brag about his kids. If they asked, he said, "I would like to keep that separate because it's personal." He didn't like to talk about his private life to the media, but this was one area where I knew I was different. I wasn't afraid to share my story because it was real and it was my truth. I was his oldest daughter, and I was raised by my daddy's family, so I felt a real strong connection with him, always had. I was also at a place where I was able to say "I'm B. B. King's daughter, but watch this. This is my show. I do my own thing."

It was time for me to take a bow and thank those nice folks for coming out to hear me sing and cut up for a bit. That night had been a rollercoaster ride for my emotions, but with as much as I'd been through, that wasn't nothing. Besides my own issues, I still had to deal with negative stories about Daddy, people asking me for favors or thinking I had lots of money, and those who were running Daddy's business affairs telling me I didn't have the right to use my own father's name. That was a helpless feeling, I can sure say that much.

Once I got off stage and made my way back home to Chicago, I was gonna tell my whole story and I wasn't going to stop until I was done. I'd seen how not sharing with others could come back to bite you in the behind. I think that's one of the things my daddy got wrong. He should have been more open, more vocal, and maybe more nurturing. He was a reserved, quiet, humble man, and nobody knew that better than I. I will always respect and love him, but I was determined to change the direction of my life before it was too late.

The first thing I was going to do was share my story, and I'd be damned if someone was going to tell me that I couldn't talk about my own daddy, because that's just what I was going to do.

Well, maybe after one more sip of that sweet Blues Juice.

CHAPTER 2 – ARKANSAS

I was born on October 26, 1949, at around five or six in morning. My mother was living in a rural part of Arkansas called Gilmore, about thirty miles outside of West Memphis. Her name was Mary Elizabeth Jackson. She was nineteen when she had me, after she had met a young man named Riley B. King. She said what attracted her to him, besides his good looks, was how considerate he was. He was always very charming and polite, even as a young man, and Mama responded to that. She was sweet on him right from the jump. My mama was a very attractive young woman and very well proportioned, too.

Riley King had been working in a few juke joints and small clubs in the area trying to get that music thing going. Mama was known around those parts as a real good cook. People would rave and carry on about everything she made, even her bologna sandwiches. They just loved whatever she put together, so to make a little money, she helped out in the kitchens at a few of these juke joints.

That's where she met that charming musician. There were other girls around, too, all trying to catch his eye, but Mama told me later that she was not interested in getting messed up in all of that. After his set one night, that musician moved past the other young ladies and made his way to Mary.

"Hi, I'm Riley."

"Hello."

That was it. As was often the case back then, her mother, my grandmother, didn't take it well when her daughter came home with the news that she was pregnant. She wasn't happy when Mama started hanging around with Daddy in the first place, being that he was a struggling musician and all, but Grandma really didn't like that there was going to be a baby and, apparently, no marriage. That was something my church-going grandmother couldn't understand. *How you going to be with child before you get married? Life is too hard out here as it is.* She was just worried that her daughter would have to struggle.

As for Daddy, he was born in 1925 in a small town called Berclair, Mississippi, in a little ole house on the plantation, where his father, Albert, worked. After his mama, Nora King, died, he was raised by his grandmother and other family members. He worked in the fields as a child, and went to school when the crops were done growing. My great-grandmother died when he was in his early teens, and that's when my grandfather, Albert, came back into the picture. He took Daddy to live with him in Lexington, and that's where he went to school. He said he always had a rocky relationship with Albert. I found out, when I lived with him later on, that he could be a difficult man to be around.

Eventually, Daddy married a lady named Martha Denton, and started singing Gospel music in a group. Around 1946 or so, three years before I came into this world, he moved to Memphis, Tennessee, with his cousin, Bukka White, who was a Blues singer. I guess things weren't happening fast enough for Daddy and his music, so in 1948 he came to West Memphis, Arkansas, just over the state line from Memphis. That's where he started performing on Sonny Boy Williamson's radio program, which was very popular at the time. He was building a name for himself locally and word was beginning to spread throughout the South about him—this new singer that they called "Beale Street Blues Boy," then "Blues Boy," and finally just "B. B."

During Daddy's run on the radio show, with his reputation building, he met my mom and they hit it off. Mama was smitten right away, and I'm sure the music element didn't hurt, either, but she realized real quick that she would probably never be the only woman in his life. With his popularity growing, there were lots of pretty young ladies coming around. Mama was no exception, but there was one difference: she was pregnant with his child, and that would connect them for life. After I was born, Mama set off to raising me with her family around her, and my Daddy coming by when he could. With the demands of his growing career and a job that meant playing in clubs late at night, he didn't have a lot of time to spare.

My mama and daddy remained friends, and it was a pattern he would follow for his entire life. He promised any woman that he was involved with that he would stay in her life forever. At first, these women were excited, because, to them, it meant maybe there was hope that one day they would eventually get back together with him. However, after he had more children, Daddy explained to me that he decided never to marry a woman he got pregnant because that would negatively affect his other children, whose mothers he hadn't married. It was a different kind of logic, but it worked for him, and he did stay true to his word. Not only that, he was always generous with his former loves.

My mama lived with her mother and raised me with the help of nearby family. She also did some housecleaning to make a little money to contribute to the household. By the time I was two-and-a-half years old, my mother had met and married the man who would become my stepfather, Curtis Lee Gilmer. He was very good to me and my mother. He had a nice job, and that meant Mama only had to do odd jobs to pick up extra money, like occasionally cooking, since she enjoyed that so much.

I've always had a very clear memory. For some reason, I can recall things from way back like it was yesterday. I remember when I was just three years old that I knew my father was an important man. I was living with my mama and her new husband, and when Daddy came around, there was an electric charge in the air, a feeling of excitement that is hard to describe. I knew his visits were something special. His career was picking up and people were starting to take notice. He was dressing the part, too, wearing nice clothes and taking care of his hair. He was still doing manual labor, like working in the fields, to make some money while he played music on the side, but we could all tell that he was going places. Even at that young age, I wanted to go with him.

Now Mama and Daddy had such a good relationship that he came by when he could to visit me, and he would, of course, help us out financially. I don't know why, but I had an instant connection with him. I loved my mama and all, but Daddy and I were very much alike and we just clicked. Any time Mama told me he would be coming around, I got dressed up real pretty and waited patiently, making sure not to mess up my clothes. If he was late, I pestered Mama. "When is he coming? Where is Daddy?" I tried to be good, but it was hard. After my mama had remarried, things changed a little bit.

One day, Daddy came over and, even though I was just a little girl, I could feel the tension. I was sent in the other room, and the three of them sat around the kitchen table talking. Of course, I strained hard to hear what they were talking about. They were calm and no one yelled, but I knew it was serious. It seems they were working out when Daddy could come over and how they would deal with it. These two proud men had to come to an agreement about how I would be raised, and finally that's what they did. My stepfather certainly understood how important it was that I got to spend time with my father whenever he could make time. It was a little different because he couldn't keep a regular schedule. Daddy was working hard on his music and could only come over when he could get away from the demands that were starting to build.

Of course, I need to give credit to Mama, too, because she was caught in the middle between the handsome musician that she immediately fell for and the stable family man she ultimately decided to be with for the rest of her life. She knew that we all needed to get along to make this work, and she sincerely helped to make that happen. If Daddy didn't come around for a while, she knew how to get in touch with him. She made it a priority that I got to see Daddy because she saw how I changed when he came around. I lit up and ran into his arms. She told me she could see the bond between us.

Even while I was still a little girl, if he couldn't come to visit, Mama took me to some of his shows at the local juke joint or an outdoor picnic. Sometimes, she would leave me with my dad and his group of people so that I could visit for a while. I sat in a chair just studying him, watching his every move as he performed. I always had a big grin on my face and I couldn't take my eyes off of this magnetic man who was my father. Once he finished his show, he put his guitar down and spent time with me.

He came over, knelt down, and put his arm around me. "Baby, where your mama at?"

I smiled real big. "I don't know." I didn't really care, either. This was my time with Daddy and I was going to enjoy it for as long as I could.

He was always very protective of me, so he made sure I was taken care of if he had to go tend to business, like meeting fans or talking to other folks in the music business. He was getting more popular and he was always such a worker that his career just kept picking up steam. He wouldn't slow down for Mama or even me, and I could see that a lot of people wanted his time. He was married to his music and I learned to respect that just like everyone in his life had to do. Watching him perform planted the seed for my own music career. In fact, I started having dreams about doing the same thing. We were so much alike that I could picture myself on stage just like he was. It seemed very natural to me.

This visitation-type arrangement worked out for a few years. I lived with Mama, and it was really nice how my Daddy and step-father were both considerate of the fact that I was his daughter and that it was only fair for him to have a connection to me. I think my stepfather did feel somewhat protective, especially of my mother, and probably a little jealous. Regardless of that, the two men were never mean to each other, at least I never saw any of that. In fact, it was just the opposite. One time, my stepfather got into a bad car accident and wasn't able to work for a while. It was hard for him because he was the provider and the man of the family. Daddy heard what had happened and he came over one day with a car full of groceries for us. He was always doing things like that when he could. That's what I mean by everyone having such a good relationship. They were so respectful, and that was good for me. The only problem was that I wanted to see my daddy more often.

I was getting older and that meant I'd be going to school soon. My dad came over to have a talk with my mama, and you know that little pitchers have big ears. I crept over to the doorway so I could listen to the adults talking again like they had before. It must be serious.

Mama said something like, "I agree that she needs to be in our life, but you got that crazy schedule, late nights and all."

"We can work something out," Daddy said.

That made me smile.

"And to make matters worse, you and your family have moved over to Memphis. That's going to make things a little more difficult," Mama told him. My stepfather stayed out of it, and rightly so.

"I've got an idea," Daddy said.

Finally, they came to an agreement. I would be able to spend the school year with Daddy's family in Memphis and then come back to Arkansas for the summer to be with Mama. That way, I'd get to see Daddy whenever he was in town and I'd be surrounded by his other family members, who would make sure I was fed and clothed and going to school.

I could barely keep the smile off my face when they told me what they had decided. I didn't want them to know I had been listening. To me, it sounded wonderful. It didn't feel like I was leaving Mama; it felt like I was going to see Daddy even more, and then I could tell Mama all about it over the summer. I was one excited little girl.

When it came time to go, I packed up my stuff in a small, beat-up suitcase that Mama borrowed from somebody in the family. My mother loved to drive, so we hopped in her car and headed off to my new home for nine months out of the year. Turned out it wasn't too far away, just a few hours. So, if I needed her, she could get to me without too much trouble, but I was sure everything would be just fine.

"Now I want you to behave yourself," she told me during the drive.

"Yes, Mama."

She smiled. "These are your kin and they are taking you in, so I don't want you causing them trouble, you understand?"

"I won't. I'll get to see Daddy, right?"

"Yes you will, baby."

With that, I moved into the modest house that was run by my daddy's father, my grandfather, Albert. Daddy's three sisters also lived there, and the middle one, Cora Mae King, would be my main caregiver. She and Daddy always had a close connection, sort of like he and I had. There were just certain family members that gravitated to each other, so this seemed like it would be a good idea. Actually, I really didn't care who was watching me as long as I got to see Daddy, and that's the truth.

Since money was tight and people had to make do to get by, other family members moved into the house and some others left. That's what folks did back then, they made room for each other, because it was all about families taking care of their own. There was one time that Daddy's stepmother and her family moved in with me, my aunties, their kids, and my grandfather. It was a lot of people, but we all managed to live together.

During the summer when school was out, my Auntie Cora Mae would get a break from watching me since I was back at my mama's house in Arkansas. I got to see my mama's side of the family, which I liked, too.

There was one other thing I also liked when I went home during the summer, and his name was Booker. He and his family lived nearby and they were friends with my family. His mother and mine were very close, and I played with his sister. Since the age of around seven or eight, I was infatuated with "Book," as everyone called him. Of course, we were real innocent, but I just had that little girl dream of marrying this sweet brown-skinned boy one day. It would be a little different from the way my family was doing things then. Instead of it being the man on stage, I would be the one in show business. I had it all planned out in my young mind.

Despite my attraction to that little Romeo, there were actually some summers where if I didn't feel like I'd been able to see Daddy enough, I'd ask Mama if I could just stay there in Memphis, hoping he might come by when he got done touring. I loved my mother very much, but I didn't want to miss Daddy coming to town, and she always understood. A couple of years after I started staying over in Tennessee, she had another child, so she was busy with her new family anyway.

The King house was not grand at all. It was very basic, just three bedrooms and one bath, and just a tad over 800 square feet. It didn't feel too bad to us, because we were used to it, but there was never a lot of room to move around. In fact, sometimes it did feel like a schoolhouse, because of all the kids running and screaming as my aunties tried to keep everyone under control. The house is still there on Hubert Avenue, in an area called North Hollywood. My older stepbrother is living there to this day. I have fond memories of being there, because, even though we weren't rich at all, there was love there and we lived happily in that small, humble house.

That was the first house my father bought for the family once he made some real money, around 1952. I went to the elementary school down the street. My best girlfriend, Charlene, lived next door and we got to be very close because we were around the same age. I had a pretty good childhood life. Sometimes, not having my father around made me sad, but I knew eventually I would get to see him so that made me very happy. That gave me something to look forward to.

It wasn't all peaches and cream living there among the King family. For some reason, my grandfather was very mean to me, but he was like that to everyone. I tried to figure out why he was so angry by asking my daddy. He explained that his father never knew his mom and dad, and was raised as an orphan, so he never really understood how folks was supposed to act and interact with family. Throughout his life, Daddy said his father never told him he loved him. I can't imagine what that would do to a child. I think that had a big effect on him, because Daddy constantly told us he loved us as soon as he walked in the door and just before he left. Daddy had it tough, because his mother passed away, and then his grandmother died, as well, leaving him with just his father, who we all knew was not the man to mess with unless you wanted to get a beating.

My father was famous in the South before he was known nationally, so he already had a name by the time I was going to school. As word spread and more people heard of him, they found out that I was his daughter. The kids often made fun of me and teased me. "Why don't you go live in Hollywood?" "Don't you have any fancy clothes?" You know, petty things that little kids say to each other.

Around the second grade, I started singing and dancing. Anything that had to do with show business I really enjoyed. What I did was have my family gather around the living room, adults in the chairs and kids sitting cross-legged on the floor. I had my cousin, Walter, act like he was playing an instrument, and all the little cousins were the audience. I was the "big sister" of everyone and they pretty much did what I told them to do. That's how we spent our time. We didn't have a lot of toys, but we had each other, so we made our own fun by pretending we were in show business. Of course, I got that idea from going and watching my dad.

Sometimes, my auntie took me to my dad's shows and I sat and waited until he finished performing, just like when Mama took me to the juke joints back home. I sat on stage and watched these performers, and I was just amazed by them. To see Jackie Wilson sliding across the floor singing and dancing and putting on a show. Sam Cooke came out and he was more laid back, but his voice was tremendous. James Brown, Gary U.S. Bonds, and so many others. During that time, a show was like performance art. There were dancers, singers, comedians; many different acts put together to appeal to everyone.

As I got a little older, I started to appreciate all of the showmanship and pure spectacle that played out right in front of me. I understood that I was very lucky to see these talented new acts sharing a stage with Daddy. I was at the show one night, when I was around nine or ten years old, and I saw this lady walk out on stage. I was mesmerized. I literally gasped at how gorgeous she was. Until then, all I had seen were men, and I'd never really given it much thought, until I saw this vision. She had platinum white hair and high yellow skin, so light and pretty. She was really built with a very curvy body and she was wearing a beautiful sparkly gown. I knew right then that I wanted to be like that lady. I didn't at that time know who she was, but I knew that was my future. I could just feel it in my soul.

I went to Daddy after the show. "Daddy!"

"How did you like it, pretty girl?" He always called me "love" or "pretty girl," something like that.

"I loved it, but who was that fancy lady with the white hair?"

"Why, that is Miss Etta James."

That's all I needed to know. After seeing her and realizing that a woman really could be up on that stage with those men and be just as good or even better, I was hooked. I went home, put on my best dress, and slid pins in my hair to gather it up in fancy swirls. As I stood there admiring myself, trying to see how much I looked like the lady on stage, I saw that I had a little stomach, a child gut. I didn't have the shape that I had seen on stage and the dress didn't look quite right. I kept shifting it and moving it around, but it didn't work no matter what I did to it. It made me very conscious of my body, and I was suddenly aware of how I looked to others. I started focusing on my weight and working to get in better shape. I wanted to look like the fancy lady on stage and it didn't matter what it took to get there. That was my goal. She was everything I knew I could be.

As I worked on my weight and my body shape, I kept practicing my singing by watching myself in the mirror so I could see what the audience would see. I watched my expressions so I could understand how to make them work for me and the song. When it wasn't right, I did it over and over and over. It didn't matter how long it took. I was very determined to have a life on the stage. I knew it was just a matter of time. When I got that chance, I was going to be ready, well, me and my baby.

No, I don't mean my real baby—I had a little cousin about two years younger than me—and for some reason I just connected to that boy. I took care of him like he was mine. He was such a pretty baby. I don't know why I attached myself to him, but I did like being responsible for somebody else. At that time, as far as I knew, I didn't have any brothers or sisters. Later, I found out that Daddy had two other children, by two different women, the same year that I was born, and there were others. Plus he was still married; he had not divorced that first wife. I tell you that got a little crazy when I found out and I did feel some type of way, but I was the one living with the King family, so I took some comfort in that.

Soon, my little cousins were calling Daddy "Uncle B," so I started to do the same thing. He didn't have any problem with that, but he always came over and let me know I was his daughter. I kept that up for a minute, and then I went back to calling him the only thing that really felt right . . . Daddy.

CHAPTER 3 – JUKE JOINT BABY

During the 1950s, while the King family was making a decent life in that little house on Hubert, Daddy's career was starting to take off. He had divorced his wife and was focusing full tilt on his career. That meant that I didn't get to see him as much as I wanted to. I had to make peace with that, because it wasn't going to change. His songs started to climb up the charts and, of course, we heard them through the static of our local AM radio stations. He was doing the Blues mostly, but they were also on the R&B tip, and that made them more radio friendly.

I'm sure his career was planned out, but I was a little girl, so I didn't know a lot about that. I just remember hearing Daddy's voice coming out of that scratched up little radio and being mesmerized. It felt almost like he was in the room, like he was there with me. There were songs like "Whole Lot of Love," "Every Day I have the Blues," and "Sneaking Around," and they kept on coming. I don't know if they were playing all over the country or not, but in the South those songs were hits, and so was Daddy.

When the song "Sweet Sixteen" came out, it felt like a bigger, more wide-reaching song than the others. I was always thinking about what he was recording and how it was being received by the people. I listened to the DJs talk about the songs and I heard what folks in the neighborhood and kids at school had to say. Since most of them knew who I was, they told me things like "Oh, I like your daddy's new song a lot!" or "Why don't he do some more Blues? I could write a better song than that one I heard yesterday on the radio."

Everybody always got an opinion, and I guess they told me because they thought I'd pass it along to my dad. They felt like they had a way to get to him. That definitely took a minute to get used to and it formed a pattern that has continued throughout my life. People have always approached me with their big ideas and thoughts on music in general and Daddy's career in particular. Even as a little girl, I started to realize that you never know what folks have on their mind when they try to be your friend. At first, I enjoyed the attention that his popularity brought to me. Kids wanted to be my friends, adults wanted to talk to me, and my lady teachers gave me that knowing look. I knew what they wanted.

That made it harder for me to determine who my real friends were, because from that time on, I was continually approached in different ways. There were the casual folks, who would talk to me about all kinds of stuff they thought I'd be interested in, and then finally the subject changed to my father; it never failed. Others didn't even try to be cool about it. They just came right out and said, "Can you introduce me?" or "Will you give him this?" meaning a hand-scrawled note or poorly typed-up letter.

Like anyone, I really liked the attention, but soon I realized what was behind it and that started to get to me. In the beginning, I was the popular girl and everyone wanted to talk to me. Then, that changed, and I started to feel defensive and guarded. It went from being excited to have a new friend to wondering what they wanted from me. There were some instances where a kid just wanted to be friends, like Charlene from next door. She and I got along real good and did everything together. That was a true friend. Others, who had been friends for a while, started to change as B. B. King got more popular. Even they would ask questions about him, things they had never brought up in the past. It definitely put me on guard and gave me a taste of the other side of being famous. It was not all nice clothes and fancy houses.

Speaking of houses, when I was about ten years old, back in 1959, we were all playing outside in the backyard when Aunt Cora Mae pushed open the squeaky screen door and yelled at us. "You kids come on inside. Uncle B is here and he wants to talk to us. He said he has some news!"

"Daddy!" I screamed, and pushed my way inside.

There were still a lot of us living there, so I had learned that it was up to me to make sure I got a good spot on the living room floor. I waited for weeks and weeks for one of his visits, so I was sure not going to waste it. Out of respect, the adults got the spots on the sofa and the assorted chairs, but I found my place on the floor, front and center. Then, I jumped up, because I almost forgot to hug Daddy first. I asked my cousin to save my spot and then ran over.

"I missed you so much," I told him as I squeezed him real hard.

"Aw, I missed you too, pretty girl," he whispered to me during our hug.

I made a beeline back to my place in the center of the room before it got taken by one of those other sneaky kids, because you learn to look out for yourself in a family that size. Someone had left a chair in the middle of the room for Daddy. After everyone said their hellos, they all got situated and turned the floor over to Mr. B. B. King.

"I'm so glad to see everyone and it's sure nice to get a break from touring, I can tell you that," he said as we all smiled up at him. "And I love coming here and seeing all my kin. It's good to have a home base to come back to. I bought this house back in 1952 and it is a real good place to be, but I got to thinking, y'all don't have enough room here."

I wasn't sure where he was going with all this talk, but my eyes got big as saucers when he started counting out stacks of money on the floor right in front of me! My heart about jumped out of my chest! I never saw a whole lot of money, except on TV. These green pieces of paper didn't even look real. Looked to me like some play money from a game or something. Maybe Daddy was joking with us.

"I've been working real hard to make sure everybody is taken care of, so I'm going to use this money to get us a farm where everybody can live and there will be more room to move around. Y'all like that idea?"

We were excited to hear the news. We would move to a farm! I saw plenty of farm land and country when I went to Mama's house in the summer to visit, so I kind of liked being here where it was different. It was nice having close neighbors and stores nearby, but the country would be good, too. While the adults kept talking excitedly about the new plans, I just kept looking at all that money on the floor. My goodness it was hypnotic. I watched as Daddy carefully counted out each stack and lined them up to show how he was going to pay for the farmhouse.

My grandfather was almost smiling for once. He was working at Firestone to bring money in the house to help with the bills. He got off work at three in the morning, and if we had done something bad that day, we prayed that it didn't get reported to him. He could be a vicious spirit. You better not push the wrong button with him. Aunt Nora Fay, my daddy's oldest sister, was the one exception. She could get away with just about anything. I think he treated her special, because it was said that she favored my father's mother, who had passed on by that point. She often got a pass, but not the rest of us.

Grandfather was a proud man and a workaholic, which is probably where Daddy got it from. I had heard the stories about him growing up on a plantation, and he talked a lot about how he loved working the land, riding on tractors, and all of that. His wife, my step-grandmother Mama King, was sitting beside him the day Daddy said he was going to buy a farmhouse. She helped run the household and was almost as strict as he was, but not quite as mean. She didn't have his temper. Everything we did seemed to set him off, but she was more understanding. Don't get me wrong, she had a lot of rules for us to follow, but if we did as we were told and minded her, then she was good to us. I learned at a young age to cling to Mama King when necessary because she was the only one who could calm my grandfather down when he was on a rampage. She wasn't always successful, but if there was anyone who could do it, she was the one. She was my ticket to getting out of trouble. The beatings were always worse without Mama King around, believe that.

I think my dad was always trying to please his father and prove to him that he was a success. I guess it's a natural thing for a child to want his parent's approval, and I always felt that's what Daddy was doing, trying to impress Grandfather King. It was probably more important because of the music thing. It was risky from the start and not a whole lot of people, especially our kind of folk, made a real living at it. That might be why Grandfather kept working at Firestone. He was making sure that there was at least one income for the family just in case that music thing didn't take off. Now with all that money lined up on the floor, it was cold hard evidence that my daddy had done it. He had made something of himself and was able to buy a farm just like Grandfather always wanted.

As I was sitting on the floor, the little devil in me tapped my shoulder and got my attention. I was staring at that money and thinking, *If I had money, real money, then I would have lots of friends and everyone would really love me.* There was one stack of bills that was real close to me—right by my leg—so close that I think I could smell it. I reached over and tried to be oh so casual as I eased it right under my thigh and sat right on it. It was like a game of finders keepers. Since I had claimed this money, it would be mine and life would be different. I would be rich and those kids at school would be my friends because of me, not because of my daddy. That's how my crazy little mind was working. It doesn't make a lot of sense now that I think about it, but, of course, back then my world was very small.

Satisfied with my little game, I looked around the room to make sure no one was paying me any attention, and they weren't. Cora Mae was talking to her sister. My grandfather was talking to Daddy about his ideas for a farm, and they were making plans to go see a few properties. My cousins were not looking at me, either. Then, I saw Mama King and she had me in her sights. Her eyes were focused on me, and I mean she was giving me the evil eye. I had been made! The jig was up and I knew better than to get her mad at me. I needed her to be on my side to protect me, so I couldn't afford to do anything that went against her. I looked back at her just to make sure and she was still staring at me. Hard.

I knew she would give me a whipping if she had to, and she was pretty rugged when she wanted to be. She was a whipper if it came to that. Just as I had slid it under me, I eased myself away from that stack of money and tried to make it look like it had all been a mistake. I made sure she saw me move far away from it. I don't know what got into me. I knew it wasn't right, but I had done it anyway. I started feeling real bad, but Daddy stayed for a while and we had a nice meal, so I began to feel better.

Daddy finally said his goodbyes and gave me a real nice hug. "You be good, baby. I will see you soon, okay?"

"Okay, Daddy," I said. Like always, I didn't want to let go. I held on for as long as I could. Sometimes, I counted to see how high I could get before he let go. Finally, he pulled loose and made his way out the door. I got up to eight with that one hug.

I started to go back outside to play, but Mama King grabbed me by the arm and yanked me into an empty room. She told me that stealing was a real bad thing do to. She said if something wasn't mine, I had no right to take it. "If you ask for something and someone gives it to you, that's a different story, but you do not take from others." She also stressed the importance of family. She said we had to depend on each other and you never break the trust of family and you never, ever steal from each other. "Stealing is just plain wrong."

I learned an important lesson. I knew it was wrong, but seeing how angry Mama King was made me understand how serious it was. She was really upset that I had even considered taking advantage of family. Being together and supporting each other was how we survived. We couldn't turn on each other. That was something Daddy always stressed to us as well. We have to look out for each other and we never take what we didn't earn or what wasn't given to us. I would never forget that.

There was nothing I would do to jeopardize my relationship with my father. It was hard enough to get time with him, so I'd never purposefully mess that up. In fact, I used to ask him to stay with me until I fell asleep. He walked me to my bed and climbed in with me, staying there until I finally nodded off. I felt so happy and secure when he did that. It was our special time. Then, I woke up, and he was gone, and I had to be back under my grandfather's rule. I was always careful not to get him upset at me.

It took about a year after that big announcement for Daddy and my grandfather to find a place to buy out in the country. Once they did, we were on the move. The idea was for all of Daddy's kin to be able to live together and for him to come and stay there when he wasn't touring. I didn't think that would ever happen because, number one, he was always touring, and number two, he didn't really want to be living among all of us. He was used to having his lady friends, especially when he was on the road. A regular home life was just not for him.

The farm was real nice, with lots of land for animals and crops. It was in Bartlett, Tennessee and sprawled along almost 150 acres. In addition to the main house, there were sheds, outbuildings, tractors, and everything. This was different from the farms back in Arkansas, because there it was usually the Black folks living on a plantation that they had to work during the day. It was a matter of convenience for the owners. They had their help living right on the property.

Back then, it was rare for a Black family to actually own a farm on their own, but that's what we did. We worked it just as my daddy and grandfather had done growing up, although, this time, it was to clothe and feed us and make a better life for everyone. I remember the first time I saw the place. There was land and corn fields as far as I could see. The minute we moved over there I could see a change in my grandfather, too. I could tell he was excited to get back to the farming life. He also seemed very proud that this was family land that his son had bought with his own money. Best of all, there was more room for more people. My aunties and their kids moved in, and a cousin from Mississippi showed up. A lot of people went back and forth, but with more room, it felt better. It also helped that we all worked on the farm and contributed together. It helped to build our family bond.

The one bad thing about living on the farm was that we had to walk about eight miles to get to school. Not only that, each morning we had to feed the cows, pigs, and chickens first. I can't forget the turkeys. I did not like them at all because they were mean. They would peck at me, so I tried to stay as far away from them as I could. After our chores, we got dressed and walked down a dirt road to school. Mama King made sure that all of our clothes were clean and we had nice lunches. Since there were a few of us in school, we made the walk fun by goofing off and being silly, but we always made sure to get to school on time. Mama King would not be happy if we missed first period. I'll admit there were a few times that we heard the bell and started running, but we usually made it.

During this time, Daddy still came to visit, and those are my favorite memories. On one of those visits, this pretty lady named Ruby was there. She lived just down the road about a quarter mile from us. Every time he was there, she showed up, so I started putting it together that this was his new lady friend. It was surely no secret that a lot of women around there wanted to meet my daddy and try to win him over. The more popular he was, the bigger catch he became. Plus I think he was getting a reputation as a ladies man. When he did decide he liked someone, she was always very beautiful with a nice figure, just like Ruby.

I learned to gravitate toward the new woman in his life, because I realized early on that if she took to me, I would be more welcomed when Daddy came around. I didn't want to create any roadblocks to seeing him, so being friends with his lady meant there was no threat from me. Plus, in my silly dreams, I thought maybe one day the three of us would be a real family. I always felt incomplete living between the two homes, especially when there was no guarantee if or when my father would show up. So, that made it tough for me to feel like part of a family unit. I definitely had a large extended family, but sometimes I just wished it was only us and no one else taking my "daddy time" away from me.

If he loved a woman, then I liked her. That was my survival strategy and it worked for a while. Of course, we never did have that small family that I dreamed of. In fact, our family on the farm just kept on growing. Those sisters, my aunties, kept having more and more kids. What made it even crazier was that Cora and Bernelle would have them around the same time so that would be two new babies at once. Since I was the oldest, I was usually the designated babysitter. That cycle went on for maybe six or seven years. I was enjoying the farm life, but I was getting tired of taking care of animals and children. It felt like I was far removed from the entertainment world that I had dreamed about. I wasn't even able to see as many of my dad's shows because he was starting to travel farther away as his popularity grew. I was yearning for something more.

My summers back in Arkansas were a nice break for me because of a few things. First, there weren't as many babies around, so it was a little easier on me. I did take to babysitting at first, but after all those years it got tiresome. I was still a kid myself. Not only that, but I got to see Book, and that was always special for me. Once I got something in my head, I just couldn't let it go, and this was one of those times. I just knew Book and me was going to be married one day and have our own little family with a mom, dad, and a couple of babies. Actually, after all that babysitting, I wasn't too excited about having my own kids, but we would have to see about that.

The other thing I liked during the summer were the juke joints. Mama still worked at them on the weekends, because it was just in her nature to cook for folks, and that's what they wanted, too. I think she liked the attention and appreciation that came with it, not to mention a little folding money. On Friday and Saturday nights all across the South, juke joints came alive with singing, dancing, and good food a-cookin'. After working in the fields all week, folks were ready to let off a little steam. So, on the weekends they went home, took a nice tub bath, and headed to the nearest joint for some cuttin' up.

For Black folk, that's where most of our music was played. Some were on the radio, but if we wanted to hear the real thing from all the young artists just coming up, then we went to the local club. Since I was home, Mama took me along with her so we could spend time together. At first, I helped out in that hot, sweaty kitchen, but once I heard the band start to play those first notes, I was headed for the main room.

The clubs were real basic, nothing too fancy, and they often had a similar setup. There was one area to sit and eat that good home-cookin', another area for a little bit of gambling, and then, of course, the main area, where the shows and dancing happened. Matter fact, a lot of early Blues musicians toured the circuit working for free food and tips from the audience, just as B. B. had done.

As a kid, I always wanted to go to new places and try new things, and I often dragged my cousin, Frager, along with me. She always called me "feisty" and knew that I was always looking for an adventure. All the bands played in the joints across the railroad tracks, and since we were little, we were not allowed to cross over to that side by ourselves. We were supposed to hang around outside of Fred's café, but, of course, I convinced Frager to sneak over there, and once we did, we were hooked. We found something to stand on and peeked in the windows. Seeing those folks sweating, swaying, and laughing was an exciting feeling. It was like we had stumbled upon a wonderful secret world, and I was under its spell. We went home and danced in front of the mirror trying to mimic the Hawaii hula dance we'd seen on TV. I discovered that I was able to move my stomach like nobody else.

My stepfather had a little money and opened a small joint where Mama would cook the meals. There was no age restriction, so it wasn't unusual for some young kids to be running around as long as someone was minding them. Most of those places were dimly lit and filled with lots of cigarette smoke in the air. The windows were propped open to try and catch the rare summer breeze and cool everyone down just a little so they just might stay longer and spend more of that cotton money they had earned. We were in a small town, so when someone we had heard of came by, it was big news. I remember Little Junior Wells came through that small Arkansas town when I was young.

After I watch a few of the performers, I got an idea: I went to the kitchen with Mama, and after she got busy cooking, I made my way into the dining area. I saw the people sitting and eating and I just started to sing and dance. At first they didn't pay me much attention, but then they started getting quiet, watching the little girl in the corner of the room. It started off very innocently. I just wanted to see if I could put into practice the performance I'd been working on over in Tennessee. When I was done, I smiled and took a little bow. To my surprise, they started handing me coins to show their appreciation. I hadn't planned on that, but I sure did like it.

Each week after that, I'd make sure my favorite dress was clean and ready for the weekend. It was white with green flowers on it and I called it my twist dress. When I had that on, I was ready to entertain. That particular joint had a section for the Blacks and a separate one for the Whites. Once word about my shows started spreading, more and more people showed up. One night, I did my show and after I was done, I looked up and saw the White people peering over the divider to get a look at me. Now even the White people were taking notice! Plus, they gave me money, too. I knew that this was something special.

It was very interesting to me because with Daddy I saw all the popular singers who were starting to really make a name for themselves. They were polished and very professional. Then, when I visited Mama, I got to see the other side, those struggling to get a foothold in the very competitive music business. The talent was definitely equal to if not better than some of the pros I'd seen, but we just never knew if any of them would make it big. It gave me a good perspective to see the full spectrum from those just starting out, to others about to break on through and go to the top of the charts.

Mama seemed very happy with the life she had, taking care of her family and cooking on the weekends. My stepfather worked at John Deere and was able to take care of her financially, so it was nice to see her doing things just because she wanted to. He also made sure she had a car, which was a real luxury back then. She just loved her car and she loved to drive even more. In fact, since not many folks had one, they were always calling her up. "Miss Liz, I need a ride." "Miss Liz, I gotta go to the store." I was amazed at how she pitched in and helped her neighbors and kinfolk get around.

When I spent the summer with her and wasn't in the juke joint, I just rode around in that car as she ran her errands and chauffeured others. Her love of people was infectious, and it definitely rubbed off on me. I think that helped me to feel so comfortable meeting new people. I didn't feel like I was meeting any strangers. Everybody that I met was my friend—well, that is, until they did me wrong. Then, we had ourselves a problem.

Of course, everyone in the South knew about B. B. King, and his reputation continued to grow. He was known for the way he represented himself, the way he sang, his stage presence, and even the fact that he was considered a real gentleman. Of course, the women always had an eye for him. Since everyone knew he was my daddy, I got a lot of respect and, of course, a lot of questions, mostly from those ladies interested in him. Because of my situation, I didn't have to work in the fields like most of the other families and children did. My dad always told Mama that he didn't want me to live the life he lived working in a cotton field or doing manual labor. So, even though I didn't have to, sometimes I helped out picking cotton just to be around my friends. That's where everyone was during the day. I was sometimes the water girl and made sure everyone was cooled off. If it got real hot, I went home, because since I didn't work out there a lot, I wasn't able to handle it like the others could.

At the end of the day, after being out in the field, my mom began her drive around town, and I liked that part, because I watched the countryside fly by the window. Then, when it got real dark, we went home to bed, and then got up and rode some more. My stepfather was extremely good to me. He wanted me to feel love even though I wasn't his child. He put effort into making me feel wanted, and that made me happy.

It wasn't the same as being around Grandfather King. Man, he laid into me a bunch of times, but I still wanted to be near my dad, so I took that abuse. When my dad came home, I didn't dream of telling him about it, because I could see he was always trying to get his father's approval. That meant I didn't want to mess up their relationship. I usually just kept quiet about the abuse. At that time, it wasn't called abuse, but I knew it wasn't a good thing the way he beat me. I knew that if I opened my mouth, my dad's family would send me home to my mama.

When I went to elementary school, things were strange. I saw other moms and even dads come to school, meet with teachers, or attend events that were taking place. The one thing I never had was anyone there looking out for me. My aunties always made sure I was ready and got to school, but they never came to see me in one of my plays or showed support for an award I won. I guess they just had too much to do. I didn't really understand it all back then. I often heard "how lucky I was to be B. B. King's daughter," but the other side was that I was often very lonely.

I never felt like the King side was an overly loving family, but we did take care of each other, and I suppose that's the way they showed their love. There were occasions when my dad, who was supporting the house financially—well, his money went funny sometimes because he was famous, just not always "famous with money." That's a big difference. When the money was not there, I felt like people, even in the house, didn't treat me as good. I loved my family on my father's side, but some of the unfairness I didn't understand. Despite the harsh treatment and feelings of not really fitting in, I stuck it out because of my love for my father.

Out of the blue, it seemed like, Auntie Cora decide she was going to up and move to California, where Aunt Faye, the youngest sister, was living. Cora was close to her little sister and decided the change would do them both good. That left me living on the farm mainly with Daddy's new girlfriend. I didn't like that situation very much, but I learned to adjust as I always did. Daddy had taken up with a girl named Sue Carol Hall. I say "girl" because she was still in school. She was the daughter of a club owner in Indianola, Mississippi. Daddy had moved her in with us, and she wasn't much older than I was, but she was about to be my stepmother. It felt real strange, but like always, I made friends because I knew that's how I could stay close to Daddy.

Someone in the house—I don't recall who—told me that I should go on out to California with my aunts. I could work with them babysitting and cleaning houses while I went to high school. With several family members gone, leaving me there with Sue and my grandfather, I decided maybe that was the best thing for everyone. So, in just a matter of weeks, I was living out in Los Angeles and helping Aunt Cora and Aunt Faye clean fancy houses up in the Hollywood Hills, including ones that belonged to celebrities. Some of the other relatives lived nearby in Compton and downtown Los Angeles.

Not too long after that, Daddy told us that he and his new bride would be moving out to California, too, and they landed in Pasadena. In the span of a year or two, most of the family had migrated West and settled into life in the bright sunshine. Once Daddy got situated, my mind started going into overdrive again and I thought maybe they would ask me to move in with them. Sue already had a son, but if I joined them, it would be almost like a regular family with a mom, dad, and some kids in a happy home.

My new stepmother had her own ideas.

CHAPTER 4 – GO WEST

I was around thirteen, when my father agreed that I could move to California and join the other members of the family that had decided to relocate to warmer temperatures. I had certainly grown close to my aunties and their children, and it felt a little strange on the farm without them. Being there with my grandfather was not my idea of fun, especially as I was going into my teen years. I had always felt like I belonged in a city, somewhere with bright neon lights and lots of music, like I'd seen on TV. While I was in Memphis, I was involved in drama classes and music. I've always loved and felt comfortable on the stage. To me that was the greatest place to be. So, the more involved in the arts I became, the greater my desire for something more.

I listened to music all the time, and not just my father's music. Of course, I loved the way he sang and played guitar, but I was a teenager, and in my mind, the Blues was the music of my parents. Not many teens want to listen to the same music that their mom and dad like. It was just a natural process to want to assert my own independence. Plus, I always thought Blues music was so sad. I hadn't yet come to understand all of the pain and struggle that it represents. Our radio stations played a variety, not just one genre like they do today. I took to more of a Gospel sound, some Soul tunes, and even Country and Western, as they liked to call it. I was open to all kinds of sounds, as I tried to find my own way.

When I was in a play or musical, I tried to incorporate things I'd learned from the songs I heard on the radio. I tried to mimic some of the vocal styles, just experiment to see what worked best with my voice and what felt right. Any time I had a free moment between taking care of animals and little children, my focus was on the music. My teachers constantly encouraged me. Partly, it was because of my father, but there was always the assumption that little Shirley would be an entertainer.

Some of the other family members were into music, too, but no one seemed to have the focus that I did. It was real clear to everyone who knew me that entertainment was in my blood and not much could change that. I did try to focus on my studies, but to tell the truth, my heart was not in it. I'd see those kids who just love spelling, or could add and subtract like a machine. I realized early on that was not my gift. I did just fine in school, but when it came to the plays and performances, that's where my God-given gift came to light. To me, the classroom was just something to endure until I could go to play practice or hurry home to listen to the radio and practice performing in my room.

That probably disappointed Daddy a little bit because since I stayed with his side of the family during the school year, it was really his responsibility to make sure I got a good education. In fact, that became one of his goals in life. As his family continued to grow, he stressed over and over to anyone who would listen that education was a priority. He was trying to instill in us that music was not an easy path to success. As a kid, he had done back-break-ing, sweaty work in the cotton fields, so it was his hope that his children and grandchildren got a solid education and good jobs. He could not give them undivided attention, but he could provide financial support and inspire all of us to take school seriously.

That message of his sounded real good, and we all understood that learning was important, but the way it was delivered may have been the problem. While he talked about how necessary it was for us to focus on our studies, we heard him on the radio and saw him on TV living that music life. When he came home, I sat still and listened to him describe life on the road. I didn't know then that he was censoring the parts about the women he met, but it was no secret that he had a weakness for pretty ladies.

Since I took everything he said to heart, it created a little con-flict inside of me. I wanted to be real good at school and get high marks so he would be proud, but the fact was that it was not one of my gifts. I knew I would be some type of entertainer. Even my teachers could see that. It went from "make sure to study because you need to get a good grade on the test" to "that's all right, Shirley, you just hurry on home because you are the lead in the play tonight." It was clear to just about everybody that I would just get by in school and then really shine when it came to performing.

I think it was hard for Daddy to come to terms with his circumstances. He was trying to be a parent from the road and that just don't work, even for B. B. King. This was around the time that he had an idea of a way to create that family atmosphere. He was known for always traveling with a large group, each assigned a different task as they all worked to build a lasting career. Daddy realized that traveling was going to be a way of life for him, so he decided that if he couldn't be with his family, maybe he could create one on the road. He bought a huge tour bus and named it Big Red.

It made sense, because he started the almost impossible schedule of playing a gig every night, 365 days a year. It was an extreme career move and surely one of true dedication and perseverance. There was no denying that my father was married to his music, and that meant a life of travel. So having that big old bus for his whole band was a real luxury, at first, and then it became a necessity. It was the only way to keep up with that schedule. He had a dedicated driver, his bandmates, and others, who would join, such as his manager, songwriters, and all kinds of people that helped build his career.

He always liked being surrounded by people he trusted, so once they were in his good graces and had proved themselves to be someone with the same mindset as him, they were good to go. They all traveled together in that bus. I was still a little kid when they were in a terrible accident not too long after he got Big Red. I found out later that he was forced to pay out a lot of money as a settlement. That was another double-edge sword, because that meant he had to travel even more to earn that money back while still taking care of his growing family. I don't know how he dealt with that kind of stress, but he did. I guess after working in the fields under the hot sun, he learned to handle all kinds of things that life threw at him.

While Daddy kept traveling around, I finally got settled in Los Angeles and stayed with my auntie. I was enrolled in Gompers Junior High School and, naturally, the first thing I gravitated to was the drama class. This felt like a different level from the one back in Memphis. It seemed more professional, I guess because of the entertainment industry being close by. It was exciting for me, because it seemed like maybe this was a step up for me as far as performing and learning about life as an entertainer. I quickly gained a reputation as a good singer and won the lead in most of the plays. I got rave reviews, and the teachers made a big fuss over me. As you can imagine, that did not go over real well with the students who had been there longer.

They saw me as the new girl from the South, who had come in and started taking their roles away. That kind of thing was much more important in Los Angeles. In fact, I found out that this did seem like it might be a good fit for me because studies were important, but they put a real big emphasis on extra-curricular activities, too. Out there, being in entertainment was not really seen as an option; it was more like you should do that and if you couldn't then maybe you'd get good grades and still be okay. That's the way it felt to me, anyway.

While I was getting lots of attention from the teachers, and once again the female faculty in particular seemed very excited to learn I was B. B. King's daughter, the other students resented me. That made it difficult to build friendships, especially at first. It was bad enough to be new, but I was also seen as a threat so that didn't make the kids flock to me.

At home, as I had predicted, I was once again a built-in babysitter because, of course, my fertile aunties were still having those little ones right and left. I didn't really mind, because at least I didn't have to worry about trying to feed those angry turkeys back on the farm anymore. My real escape from my chores was being able to sing and dance. After a successful performance in a play, I went home feeling more inspired, but once I opened that door, reality brought me back to earth. It got to the point where I preferred to stay at school, in the echoing auditorium, where I could dream without distraction. It felt like I was being pulled in two directions—the sound of applause or the screams of babies.

One of my aunts had a housecleaning business and asked if I would like to help her. I jumped at the chance, because at least it meant getting out of the house. If I wasn't babysitting, I was help-ing clean huge, beautiful homes up and down the Hollywood Hills. I didn't mind that much, because it meant I wasn't dealing with babies all the time. It was good to get away from that for a while. Also, I got so see some stunning houses, one of which was owned by Sonny and Cher. They were just building a name for them-selves and were still working-class musicians. They weren't huge stars yet, but they did have a very nice house. Each time we went to clean it I looked around to see what was new since our last visit. I felt like I was watching their career blossom through the items they accumulated. Just being in the same house as these entertainers gave me a little jolt of excitement.

The real bonus of being out there was that Daddy had finally relocated to his place nearby in Pasadena with his new young bride. She also had her child, her brother, and her sister living there, since she knew Daddy wouldn't be around all the time. I was surprised to see that he was trying to stay in one place longer than usual, but it made sense. Since he was now in Los Angeles, there were lots of local venues where he could play that didn't require him to travel for weeks on end. Of course, he still did that, too, but I could see he was trying to hold on to his new marriage, and the only way to do that was by putting in the time. That's what a new bride wants more than anything, to be with her husband. She might have been too young to realize that, with a man like my daddy, home life was not going to come natural.

I thought, *This is great! Daddy is going to have to come home more because he got a new house and a wife!* That was exactly what I'd hoped for moving all the way out there. I knew that with his sisters around and all the clubs to play in Los Angeles, it would make sense that he'd be home more and I'd get to see him. At first, that is exactly what happened. My active little imagination started running on overdrive and I got it in my head that I could move into that new house with him and Sue. Then, I would finally have the close-knit family unit I had always wanted.

Daddy was on the road, and his opening act was a young man named Stevie Wonder. Since Daddy was trying to stay local as much as possible, he was booked for a full week at a nearby club.

That was rare for him. It was usually one night here and another there. It was a real luxury to know he would be in one place for an entire week. I told him how excited I was to see him and Stevie. He promised that I could see the show, and he kept teasing me since Stevie and I were the same age. He told me that if he let me come, Stevie might like me, but he was just being silly.

When it came time for me to go to the show, I could barely contain my excitement. My aunties helped me get dressed up, and we were finally on our way to the 54 Club (everybody called it the "five four club"). Stevie came out and he performed his big hit at the time, which was a song called "Fingertips." It was a fun song, and the boy they called Little Stevie Wonder was dazzling. The show was just wonderful. He was like someone beyond his years, because he was already a showman who could play just about any instrument. I was amazed at the talent he had. The one thing that I did not like was that he started called my father "Daddy," because he had been raised by a single mother, and I guess they started bonding on the tour. Whatever the reason, I felt a touch of jealousy when he did that in front of me.

The next day at school, I told the kids that Stevie Wonder was my boyfriend and we were going to get married. Of course they teased me for the rest of the day. They didn't even believe I'd gone to see him. I was used to that kind of thing. Many of them also doubted who my father was. So, coming to school and talking excitedly about Stevie didn't help matters. I was used to being questioned and doubted. It felt like I was always having to prove who my father was. I even considered not telling people anymore, but then I realized that would be dishonest. I'd be hiding part of myself just to avoid the hassle. I shouldn't have to do that, but it made going to school more stressful than it needed to be.

The one thing school did help with was that it gave me an escape from the trouble that was starting at home. As a young teenager, I had started to gain the attention of the men that my aunts were dating, and it was unwelcomed to say the least. Seeing this show, and having my father close by for a while week, was comforting, and seeing Stevie was not only a nice distraction but also motivation for my dreams of performing. The one thing I noticed was how adoring and proud Daddy was of Stevie. That gave me the idea that if I did the same thing, I would get that look, too.

My aunties had a long-standing tradition of cooking huge dinners for anyone and everyone who wanted to join. They kept that up after moving to California. So, with my father in town doing those shows, they offered to cook dinner for him and Stevie and anyone else they wanted to bring along. I knew them very well and they didn't fool me. I knew they wanted to do that to look important to their new friends. Not only was their brother, B. B., in town, but he was bringing over that child prodigy who was tearing up the charts! Daddy agreed that it might be nice for Stevie to be around a real family atmosphere after traveling on the road so much.

After I found out that he was definitely going to be there, I told the kids at school that not only had I seen Stevie at the club and we were getting married one day, but he was also coming to my house for dinner. Of course, they didn't believe me. So, I got an idea: I decided that to prove he was coming, I'd sell peeks for 50¢ apiece. Each kid would pay me and then get to take a quick look at Stevie as he came in the house. That would prove that I wasn't lying and I'd make a little money, too. The only catch was that they couldn't tell their parents, and they had to leave immediately after they got a look at him.

My family had learned through trial and error how to deal with having a celebrity as a relative. Each of us had to quickly assess people and try to determine their motives. It wasn't easy to do either. We were always dealing with folks who wanted to use us to get to B. B. At first, it was flattering to have people become friendly so quickly after meeting them, but each of us slowly learned that they were often looking for something more.

Naturally, Stevie's manager and bodyguard had warned us not to tell anyone about dinner because that could cause problems if word got around town that he would be at our house. They said that if they found out that we had told anyone, they would just turn around and drive away. Not even the threat of leaving stopped me from my carefully-crafted plan. I told the kids to hide around the corner of the house, and when the car pulled up, they could peek around and look at him as he came inside. Then, they would have to get on along, because I didn't want anyone to find out.

So that night, my school friends showed up and hid around the corner just as they had promised. They all stayed quiet and watched as the car pulled up and a guard opened the rear door to let Stevie out. Just then, all of the kids broke into a full run and made a beeline straight for the car, screaming all the way! Oh my goodness! It was a mess. The bodyguard got one look at the group of screaming kids, pushed Stevie back into the car, and they took off into the night.

My aunties had prepared this huge feast, and I'm sure they told everybody they knew, that's just how they were. When they realized what had happened, they knew exactly who had put together the whole thing. I got the beating of a lifetime for that one. I never heard if they told Daddy, but I'm sure he found out with Stevie traveling with him and the aunties telling him everything. He never said a word to me about it.

At one point, Daddy and his new little family even went camping. I couldn't believe that was something they would do, but they sure did. Maybe they were trying to enjoy some of the simple things like they had back down South. I tried to get invited, too, but it was no use. Sue was intent on having her own family, and I was probably just a reminder of his past, something she probably didn't want to think too much about. They told me I couldn't come along on the trip. Later, I heard one of my aunts say, "Ain't that something? Riley took that dog of his on the camping trip. I think he loves that dog more than he loves Shirley."

When I heard that, I couldn't believe it. Her comment really affected me, because I had been dealing with his absence my whole life and I thought things might get better, but this was telling me that things were still the same. It hurt more because that was my family talking like that about me. That did not feel good. After that, I fell into what I guess you'd call depression. I lost interest in school and just had a hard time all the way around. My self-esteem fell right out of its socket. I had really taken a hit with that one, so I decided I needed to find myself a boyfriend. Of course I was still thinking about Book back home, and I sent letters to my girlfriend, who would deliver them to him, but he was not here and I needed to do something.

I started to think of ways that I could get Daddy to pay more attention to me. Sometimes, I said things to my aunties that I knew they would tell Daddy. I acted up, talked back, or did other things that we were taught never to do—just to create some trouble so that my father would be called over. At that point, even negative attention was fine with me. At least I'd get to see the man I wanted so much to be like. I did try to forget my troubles and put those feelings into my school shows, but it was the same story as before. There was never anyone to come and see me or support me. I was the star of the play with no family in the audience.

Also, just like back in Tennessee, I still got teased and harassed by the other kids. "You ain't B. B. King's daughter on account of where you live." "Look at what you are wearing. He wouldn't let his daughter look like that." I could only take so much. One day, just like when I tried to steal that money, the voice inside me started talking. I started acting up even more, and when my daddy returned from that camping trip, Aunt Cora called to tell him about my mischief, but he still didn't come.

There was something in our home that Daddy didn't even know was going on when he was not around. My auntie had a boyfriend who came over a lot, and when she was out of earshot, he said things that made me uncomfortable. I was in my early teens and starting to fill out real nice, but I was learning that sometimes attention is unwanted. I was, of course, still a virgin and basically clueless on how to handle men. I respected him at first, because he was an adult, and that's what I had been taught. Things were fine, at first, but then he brushed up against me, and whispered something to me about how pretty I was, and said how nice my body looked. It took me completely by surprise, because he was an adult. It was even more disturbing because it was happening in the house where I lived, where I thought I could feel safe.

Things began to escalate to the point where I was afraid for my aunts to leave because that would mean I'd be alone with him. He reminded me often that if I told anyone, he would deny it. He also said that since he was dating my aunt, he would make sure

she believed him and not me. The horrible thing was that I knew
he was right. She was so in love with him that nothing I could say
would change that. I wasn't sure what to do, but I needed to come
up with some way to deal with it, especially when he started coming into my bedroom at night.

This went on for a long time. What started as a small annoyance
had now become an everyday reality for me. My life was not my
own. It was about power, and he was wielding it over me as he
tried to get what he wanted.

Finally, it was just too much. I remember sliding a kitchen chair
over to one of the tall cabinets and fishing around in there for
anything that seemed dangerous, or like something that could
make me sick. I collected all kind of crazy things, spices, hot sauc-
es, anything I could find, and mixed it all together. Then, I drank
it. It made me sick all right, but that was about all that happened.
My aunt saw all the contents on the counter and I finally told her
what I'd done. Daddy happened to be at his house at the time and
after my aunt called him, he came right over. He seemed nervous
for once in his life and he was smoking a thin cigar, chewing on the
end. He looked right into my eyes and I'll never forget the pain I
saw. He had deep tears welling up and I could tell he was so upset
with me.

"Why did you do this?" he asked loudly. "Why did you do this?"
I was in tears. "I don't know."

"Don't you ever try anything like that again." He never hit me,
not even a spanking, but that was the first time he'd ever raised
his voice at me. "If you want to hurt yourself, you need to go home
to your mama. She is trusting me to watch over you and I cannot
let this happen. Do you understand me, young lady?" He was so
mad he was shaking.

"Yes, sir."

That event really set the tone for our relationship after that.
He had enough of my dramatic attitude and it felt like he had really abandoned me. It was difficult because the only reason I did
anything like that was in hopes of gaining his praise, and now I had
destroyed that. It made me even sadder because hurting myself
didn't change anything. I was still forced to fight off my aunt's boy-

friend almost every day. He was relentless, even trying to touch me at night when my aunt was in the other room. It was downright scary for me. I didn't know where to turn. I couldn't tell Daddy, especially after what I had just put him through. Plus, he would just want to send me away. It was tough to realize he couldn't or wouldn't protect me when I needed it.

It had been my hope that he would somehow figure out what was happening and save me. That didn't happen, but I never tried to hurt myself again because I saw how much it affected him. I wanted him to be happy and proud of me. That was always my goal. He had gone home and apparently discussed it with his wife. Apparently my behavior really had an effect on him. I was told that he wanted me to come over and stay with them. He had told his wife that it was important that I be a part of *their* life, not just *his* life.

They agreed, and he took me to his nice house in Pasadena. I was beyond excited because this is what I had hoped would happen. Daddy would come and take me away where we could spend more time together and I wouldn't have to worry about unwelcomed advances. My dream quickly fizzed and I didn't last but a couple of days. I felt so unwelcome and out of place that I knew I could never make that my home. The coldness and distance I felt from the others was undeniable. They did not want me intruding on their lives, and I could feel it.

As I started to have romantic relationships of my own, I knew any potential boyfriend would be scrutinized by the family and especially my father. He had rules for the women in his family when it came to men. I was always trying to prove myself to him, so it was important that I got his approval. One of my aunties liked the singer Bobby Bland, and the other was friends with James Brown, but I wanted to be careful. One of Dad's rules was he never wanted any musicians or entertainers to be involved with his family, because he knew what that life was like. He was very protective and expected his rules to be followed. However, that rule became a hard one for me, because I saw so many handsome men around my dad, and, as a teenager, I thought there were many that had some good looks.

There was one man named Elmo Morris, who I thought was amazing. He looked so good to me that I quickly became infatuated with him. I was in my late teen years at that point, and when Daddy found out I liked Elmo, he was not happy about it. Nothing really happened except that I learned Daddy was serious about his rules.

I think those innocent infatuations were my way of controlling my feelings about how men usually treated me. Most were leery or inappropriate, except, of course, when Daddy was around. Nothing like that happened then, I can tell you. Finally, I reached the breaking point with the boyfriend who was pushing up on me and I told my auntie about it. I'd had enough. Just as he had threatened, he convinced her that he was not at fault. She believed him and not me, even accused me of being fast and easy. She even took me to the doctor to find out if I was still a virgin. In her mind, if I wasn't, that meant I had tricked her boyfriend into sleeping with me. It made no sense to me, but the doctor said I was still a virgin. She accepted that, but never so much as apologized for the ordeal. It was as if nothing had ever happened.

My body was a difficult thing for me to come to terms with, because I had been hoping for a nice figure like I'd seen on Etta James, but I was finding out that it came with a lot of consequences even though this was not of my doing. I fell asleep at night crying after I'd successfully fought him off once again. I just wished my dad had been able to protect me when I needed it, because it was hard when nobody would listen.

By fifteen, I was ready for a steady boyfriend, and one of my auntie's girlfriends had a very handsome son. I had a serious crush on him and hung out with him whenever I had free time. The one thing I was not going to do was give up my body. I was going to wait—maybe—until I got back East and met up with Book again. So for now, the furthest I would go was kissing and making out. That was it. I sure didn't want any more babies in my life, either. I'd been dealing with my little cousins for a long time.

By this time, my grandfather and his family had moved out to Gardenia, California. Between dealing with his temper, my aunts who didn't believe me, one of their husbands, and then a boyfriend harassing me, I was at the end of my rope. I wasn't doing real well in school, either, because my home life was too much to handle. It was very stressful.

By the time I was seventeen, I was thinking about how to get away. There were some good parts about being out in California. I was at John C. Fremont High School, and I was finally quite popular. One of the reasons for that was Daddy. He was able to play the 54 Club often, so that meant he was in town more than he had ever been. When he got local press, the kids at school told me about it. I got to go to the shows and come backstage to watch all of the action. I loved the hustle and bustle of the entertainers getting ready for their performance, the applause, the encores; I just loved all of it. Despite all of those good things, I was ready to get back to the South.

During that entire time in California, I continued to write nice poetry letters to Booker. I sent them to him or to my girlfriend to give to him. Sometimes, I called, and when he wasn't home, I asked my girlfriend to go by and check on him just to tell him I was thinking about him. Being out there with all those creepy men made my mind start to create this image of a perfect life with Book. I had known him since I was a little girl, so I knew there were no surprises. He and I got along great and we had the same dreams and values. He just felt right to me.

When I got something like that in my mind, I was like a dog with a soup bone. I didn't let go of it. That was good in some ways, like trying to get recognition in a man's business, or squaring off with a booking agent years later when he didn't pay for a show. It was bad, too. If I was too rigid and stuck in my head, I missed a lot of signs and clues. I was just tired of being in California and I longed for a simpler life, the way it was when I was coming up those summers in Arkansas. Things just seemed easier then.

Looking back, I'm sure a lot of that thinking had to do with the fact that I was getting older and facing more adult problems. I wasn't a kid anymore, and I couldn't just hope for someone to come rescue me. I sure couldn't depend on Daddy for those kinds of things. He had his own family and he was trying hard to make it work. I could see it in his actions; the way he behaved was different. He was trying hard, but it wasn't in his nature.

Even though I did like being near all of the entertainment, overall I thought California was kind of boring and Los Angeles was too spread out. I don't know why it hit me like that, but it didn't feel like the cities I had imagined. It didn't have the tall buildings, bright lights, all-night diners, people selling stuff on the corners—those where the things I wanted to experience. The city I pictured was more like New York, with a lot of action, and everybody hustling for a living. I had given this place a try, but it wasn't for me.

When I thought about the pluses and minuses, it was obvious that I needed to make a change. I would still get to see Daddy when he was touring, which we all knew would be sooner rather than later. That was another reason why a big city appealed to me. If I was there, he would probably play shows there often and I could see him then. Sometimes, with all of these new demands on him from his career and his family life, getting time with him backstage was our only real quality time. He would make a point of saying hello to everyone and being very polite and gracious, but then once that was done he would make sure to take me aside and we would have our own private talks. It became a tradition for us.

Those moments were important to me and they started to happen more and more. I think it was his way of reaching out to me at a time when I had his undivided attention. He was usually in a good mood because he'd just come off of the adrenaline rush of performing and he was always happy to see me. Throughout his life, as our careers continued, we would use that time as our own. It was special between us, something that I didn't have to share with anyone.

I called Mama with the good news. "Mama, I'm leaving California and coming home!"

"You are?" She sounded surprised. "I thought you loved it out there with the movies stars and all."

"I do, Mama, but I miss home."

She had no idea about the things I'd been dealing with and she didn't need to know. I was going to take control of my life once and for all. This time, it was my decision where I should live. I was almost eighteen and no longer a little child that could be controlled and manipulated. Things were going to be different now. I was going to take everything that I had learned so far and see if I could make myself a nice career.

I wasn't sure exactly what that would look like, but I was working on some ideas. I might go back to some of those juke joints to see some good acts and maybe even work on my own stuff. I had heard that they were not as popular as when I was a kid, but they were still a place for folks to gather and see acts on the "chitlin circuit." The times were changing, and small clubs were popping up in towns across the South. That meant that less people had use for a small, rundown, smoke-filled buildings out in a cotton field.

Music was changing, too. While Rock and Roll had lost some of its juice at the beginning of the 1960s, The Beatles and The Rolling Stones were taking over the radios and the TVs all across America. Teenagers were getting swept away in a frenzy of exciting music that stirred up feelings of rebellion and freedom. That was just the type of feeling I was looking for at the time. I needed to find my own way. I'd always have the same father, but maybe I could do something that would get folks' attention and make them take notice of this girl from the South who had developed into a talented young lady.

This move would allow me to escape some of the unpleasant things I had been dealing with that would have never changed otherwise. I knew no one was going to help me, so it was up to me to make a change. I was running away from those problems and running towards a new tomorrow that had so many possibilities for me. I could feel that things were different, the country was evolving, and the 1960s were in full swing. That was a time when people with skin like mine were fighting for equal rights, and getting them.

With all of those things happening at about the same time, I knew the time was right. My intuition told me to head back to Arkansas and see what I could get mixed up in. Maybe I could get a little act together, something like that. There was one other thing that I had left back home and now was the time to get that, too.

"Oh, and Mama, how has Book been doing?"

CHAPTER 5 – THE BODY QUEEN

My mind was made up. It became very clear to me that even though Daddy was living close by, his love for the road had won out and he was traveling in Big Red once again. The hopes of having him perform in the area worked at the beginning, but a settled home life just didn't seem to fit him. I heard talk from my aunts that his marriage was in trouble as a result, and I wasn't surprised. It was a sad fact that I had gotten used to having a drop-in daddy. He came by when he could, and he always sent for me to meet him at a show. It was becoming real obvious to me that, no matter how much I wished otherwise, this was my life and I had no choice but to accept it.

With Daddy traveling, and me taking care of babies, and the hassle of rejecting the advances of the men in the house, I was more than ready to leave the west coast. It just never appealed to me as much as I thought it would. Mama was happy for me to come home, and I was excited, too. I looked forward to reconnecting with all of my old friends and family. I also couldn't wait to meet up with Booker and rekindle the romance I'd kept alive through pretty letters and an active imagination. My heart yearned to go back home. I had one semester of high school to finish, but I couldn't take it anymore. Everyone else on Daddy's side had finally settled in California. My grandfather and that family always stayed near each other, but theirs wasn't the life I wanted for myself.

Arkansas was just as I'd left it. Not a lot seemed to change there. It was definitely a slower pace from California. I wasn't sure what my next move would be once I got settled. I just figured I'd play it by ear, see what was going on with folks that I hadn't seen for a minute. When I got into town, it was nice to see Mama again.

"Shirley, I'm so glad you're home," she said, smiling wide.

"Me too, Mama. I want to go visit the Johnsons right away. I've been talking to Booker off and on and sending him letters. Plus, I'd like to see Barbara and the rest of the family."

"Honey, there was an accident."

"What do you mean?"

Mama wrinkled her brow, took a breath, and said solemnly, "You know Mr. Johnson had a problem with the bottle. The story is that he was out late one night, and on the way home his truck got stuck on the railroad track crossing. Train ran right into him. No one is real sure what happened."

"Oh no! How is Mrs. Johnson, and is Book all right?"

"Yes, they are fine, but of course it was a real difficult time for them. After the funeral, they decided it was best to relocate."

"Where?"

"I told them they should stay, but folk going to do what they need to do. They moved up north to Chicago. They got some kin up there."

My breathing was becoming short. "Chicago? Booker? Barbara?"

"Yes, I'm afraid so."

This was not what I had planned when I pictured what it would be like coming back home. I guess in my mind everyone would be waiting on me, to welcome me with open arms. Being far away, I just had no concept of how things were in Arkansas. I guess most people think of their home as staying just the same as when they left it. That was definitely not the case for me. Mama was able to give me the Johnsons' new phone number, and I got a hold of Book. Sure enough, they were all in Chicago making a new life for themselves. My girlfriend from Arkansas, the one who took letters to Book and checked on him for me, had moved there, too. Book sounded excited to hear from me and we talked off and on over the next few weeks. It felt good to get back what I always knew we had together. We talked about all of the things young lovers do. He encouraged me to come to the city so we could try to make things work.

I said to Mama, "I think I'm going to Chicago."

"What you going to do in Chicago?"

"I'm going to get married and get a job."

I was confident. I thought I was mature. I made my own mind up, and she didn't try to stop me. Our relationship had changed since I spent most of my time with Daddy's family. We had become more like good friends than parent and child. I couldn't believe how things had worked out. The family tragedy was horrible, but they all sounded happy in their newly adopted city, and Book was eager to start up our relationship. The decision to leave California seemed like the right move for me. Everything was falling into place.

When I was finally able to get to Chicago in 1967, there was a blizzard—not just a little snow, but a real blizzard—supposedly the worst in the city's history. The snow was up to my waist. I was snowed in, and all that snow was a real mess, not to mention the strong winds.

Despite the weather, I found the city exciting and alive. I had been bored in California, and in the South, people worked all week and had fun on the weekends. I got to Chicago and found that people had fun every day of the week. They went out every single night, and live music was everywhere! I had to stay with my auntie, my mom's sister, since I didn't have a place yet. She had three boys, who were all younger than me, so it was almost like the extended family out in California, complete with small kids.

During that horrible snowstorm, I had decided I needed to see Book, but the city was at a standstill. Finally, there was a slight break in the weather and I was able get a bus and then the L to his place. I found my girlfriend, Miss Sure-I'll-Deliver-Your-Messages-to-Him, was there and no one had told me about that.

"What are you doing here?" I asked her.

"What are *you* doing here?" she replied.

The three of us had a confrontation, and she ended up leaving. It was an odd situation and I found out that the two of them had been dating the whole time I was away. The real reason Book had encouraged me to come to the city was to make her jealous. It was horrible and humiliating. After that, he and I had a long talk and he promised that it was over between them and it was time for us to start our relationship. I was happy to hear that news but scared to leave him alone after what had happened. His mom was there, and we all talked about the situation. His mom was against me staying there with the family since we were not married yet. She said I could come and visit, but I couldn't spend the night. I was hurt, because she was a close friend of my mother and she knew I was infatuated with her son.

His sister Barbara said, "Shirley, you know Mama is very religious. That will not work if you are not married."

I didn't really have anywhere to stay except over in the west side with my aunt. The hard part was my auntie's husband, who was not very nice. My aunt was basically under his control, so his word was gospel in that household. I don't think he wanted me there, but I was grateful that he didn't put me out. He just made me feel very unwelcomed. Every night, I got on the L and went to the south side to hang out with my boyfriend. We continued our courtship and I always brought it back around to marriage. I felt that he had got me to the city for that reason so it should be our focus. *We had been knowing each other our whole lives. What were we waiting for?*

He said, "I have to go and get tested for the service. If I don't get enlisted, then we can go ahead and get married."

That made me excited. I wasn't thinking about the consequences. His brother was already married and living there with the family. It just felt natural that we would do the same thing, and his mother would be fine with that. It felt like the dream was about to come true. I went back to my auntie's house because I didn't want to disrespect his mother's wishes.

He and I had a long talk about our future. I remember him saying, "If I get in, I will be away. Can you handle that?"

I said, "Sure." I thought I was so in love. I told him, "Of course I can be your wife and a faithful wife since I've loved you since I was six years old."

He decide to test me. "If you really love me, you will sleep with me."

I was still a virgin. I was saving myself for my husband. My grandmother told me, "If you give the milk away before the cow is sold then they might not even buy you." It was an old way of thinking, but I believed it and I had stuck to it through my teen years. I would only give my body to my husband. When I was performing in plays, I loved the idea of people seeing me sexually and finding me attractive, but that was different; it was an act. I wasn't giving myself to anyone except my husband. When I told him that, he acted offended and it became some sort of strange challenge.

One night, he had me meet him, and we went to his brother's new house. It was nice to see his brother and his wife starting out their life and that only fueled my ideas of marriage and happily ever after with Booker. Being away from his mother's place meant he was even more aggressive in his mission to sleep with me.

He said, "If you love me, you will do it. Why would I marry you if we haven't done it yet?"

I knew what he was trying to do. I had been pressured many times before, but the difference was that I had no interest in those other men. They didn't have a chance with me. Book was a different story, because I had pinned all my hopes and dreams on a life with him. I thought if I went through with it, this close to us getting married, then that would seal the deal. We would be together forever. So, that's exactly what I did. He was my first. That night I couldn't believe how horrible it felt. It was the most painful thing that ever happened to me. How could people actually want to do this? He seemed happy, but I felt terrible.

Despite how awful the experience was for me, at least I felt confident that he would definitely marry me now. It was like he had no choice. Two days later, he was supposed to find out about enlisting, and I was excited because I figured I'd be getting a ring either way. A lot of folk couldn't afford a big wedding back then and they'd just go to city hall. That was fine with me as long as we were together.

I called him, but there was no answer. I kept calling over and over again. I couldn't wait to find out if I was going to be a wife with a husband at home or a wife with a husband in the service. I didn't care, as long as I was the wife.

There was still no answer, so I got myself on the bus from way over on the west side in K town, and made it to the south side. It was a jump, but I was determined that we were going to see this thing through to the end, especially after that painful night. Riding on the bus, I felt like something was not right. The Spirit was telling me I was going to be hurt. I couldn't stop thinking about it.

Once I got to the house, his brother and wife were sitting on the couch . . . and Book was nowhere to be found.

"Where Book at? I'm supposed to meet him." I was excited but confused. I ignored my intuition and let the excitement take over. This was my big moment. As I looked at them, I saw they had odd expressions on their face like something was up. "Why everyone so sad? If y'all don't want to tell me anything, I will just wait here."

I meant it, too. I stayed for about five hours waiting on him to show up and commit to me. Finally, he walked in with my ex-friend and she had a big smile on her face. Turns out they had just gotten married at city hall. I cannot fully describe how hurt I was. That was the day I found out that everything in my life had been leading up to a lie. I fell apart. I had come to a new city and put up with everything for him, and then I still lost. I felt like I had the real blues.

I slowly got on the bus, and then went back to the west side and told my auntie what had happened. She started saying that she knew it would be like that.

I eventually called my mom and also told her what went down. I said that I might be coming home because I really had no reason to say.

My mama said, "You're crying now, but one day you will be happy that you didn't marry him, because he will probably turn out to have issues like his father. If that happens, you won't be able to live with him anyway."

I didn't want to hear that. I just wanted her to make me feel better. Her advice upset me even more. I kept trying to regroup, but it was not easy. The one thing that really made me even angrier was that I had given myself to him—the one thing I had promised myself would not happen—yet it did!

Because my father always kept his word, that's what I tried very hard to do. I thought that's what other people, especially men, would do. Why was it so hard to find a man who would be honest with me? Booker had lied to get what he wanted and knew all along what he was going to do. That really tore into my soul. The summer of 1968 was a very sad time for me.

I kept moving forward, because I've never been the kind to want someone who doesn't want me. I never try to hang on like some women do. If it's time to move on, I have no problem doing that.

Until I could get my money together, I stayed with a very close cousin of mine. From the end of 1968 to the middle of 1969, I stayed with her on the west side of town. We were only a couple of years apart, but she had seven kids! Seven! Not only that, she was on public assistance and living in subsidized housing. There were times when I slept and felt something on me—roaches! It was the best she could do, and I did appreciate that she allowed me there with all those kids. I was slowly learning to trust and appreciate people again.

In 1969, I went out and found my own little apartment. I was ready to do things on my own for once. I got a part-time job and started to earn some money. I was determined to not just stay in Chicago, but to make a real impact. I just wasn't sure how yet. I liked that things were going on all the time. I was meeting more and more people.

I was able to move into a hotel apartment complex back on the south side where I felt more comfortable. I also felt safer there and I made new friends quickly. The place was called the Tively Hotel and it was on 63rd and Maryland. I had a one-room studio with everything I needed—a bathroom, half-kitchen, and pullout bed—I was set up real nice.

It was a fun time for me, because a lot of other local entertainers lived there. One guy was Alan, a ventriloquist with a dummy called Hard Time. He treated that dummy just like a damn human. After a while, I started feeling like it was real, too. His characteristics were so on point that it was a little creepy, but in a fun way. It was nice to be among friends who looked out for each other. Piano "C" Red was a popular keyboardist and Blues musician and he lived there, as well. He was known all over the city.

I took to both of them and others in the building, especially those who were in show business. Alan had performances at the Grand Ballroom downtown and it was a famous place where all the social clubs held their fancy events. Alan was always booking shows over there, so I really felt connected to show business by hearing him tell stories about what happened the night before or which famous people he had seen.

I was going out a lot and enjoying the nightlife now that I was not tied down with a man or staying with a family that had a curfew. I was doing my own thing and loving it. I had met a man named Manuel Arrington, a comedian, Master of Ceremonies, and later a Blues singer. He was very connected with all the right people in Chicago, so it was good to be around someone like him. He took me with him to meet a club owner, manager, or visiting entertainer and it was great exposure for me.

One of the most popular DJs in town at the time, Herb Kent, was a friend of his. He created characters such as "The Wahoo Man" and "The Electric Crazy People." I was able to see these entertainers up close and was always around singers and dancers. That was it. I was finally in a place where I fit in with people like me. I didn't want to necessarily *be* them, but I did want to learn how to get my start in this very vibrant Black community of entertainers.

It wasn't long before I met radio station owner Pervis Spann. He was very prominent and important in the entertainment industry. If you wanted to play Chicago, you had to go through Pervis Spann, the Blues Man. He also owned several nightclubs and helped promote acts that hadn't broke through to the white audience yet, such as The Jackson 5 and Chaka Khan. The popular Black-owned radio station was WVON, and I was excited to be exposed to these popular, influential people.

By this time, my body had definitely filled out and I was turning a lot of heads. I was considered pretty and outgoing, so that helped me make friends with so many wonderful people. I fit right in with this group and knew this was where my future would be.

I was still working on getting over my relationship with Booker, and Manuel was instrumental in that. He was much more like me and we had the same interests in entertainment. We both had the ambition it takes to make your way in this tough business. It felt good being friends with someone who was so respected by everyone as a popular comedian. I really had it going on. I was in the right place and with the right people. I started living the entertainer's lifestyle. I slept during the day and focused on my career at night when the party people were out.

When I first got into town, I considered going into acting since I'd been taking classes since I was a child, but that didn't seem to be a big deal in Chicago, at least with my crowd; they were all about singing and dancing. Anyone who put out a record was considered a real star. They were going places. Getting exposure to those entertainers was invaluable to me.

During that time, my father was trying hard to make his marriage work, but it wasn't going well. When they finally split up, my dad channeled his energy back into touring and the business of making music. That's when he really started playing dates 365 days a year with the help of Big Red carting him all over the country. Most of his gigs were in Black clubs and the "chitlin circuit" where Blues was very popular. Eventually, he and his management talked about crossing into popular music. He knew that was important for a long career in the business. A lot of the Soul and R&B singers also played the Black circuit, and the city became a popular spot, especially for entertainers performing "Chicago Blues."

I found out so much about the history just by being around this group. Street musicians would play at a big flea market on Maxwell Street hoping to make enough tips to get them through another day. Then, there were house parties, and that turned into Blues clubs, which started popping up on the south side and some over on the west side, too. It was hard to realize it when it was going on all around me, but I was right in the middle of the explosion of Chicago music, and I loved it.

As the art form got more popular, the shows were taken very seriously. There were fancy clothes, polished performers, and the acts didn't just stick with singing. They added dancers, comedians, and others to enhance the experience. I suppose the goal was to keep folks entertained and that meant they would stay in the club and spend their hard earned money. In the past, when I went to Daddy's shows, he had started working in higher-end clubs, so I never really saw the gritty side of the Blues scene until I got to Chicago.

One of the benefits of becoming friends with this group was that they also either interacted with my dad or wanted to, so they were very welcoming to me. When Daddy came to play, he often worked with Pervis, who even acted as his manager for a while, so it was all in the family. Daddy started playing in town so much that people thought he lived there, but he never did. He just kept on traveling, mostly in the South and Midwest. Booking agents approached him with jobs all the time, because they knew his reputation as being trustworthy and able to generate good crowds. He wasn't making a lot of money, but he was still working steady and building a following.

Watching him helped me learn how to conduct business and how to behave in an industry that was filled with more than its share of con men and scammers. Especially being female, it was a struggle for me to get respect as a new performer. Seeing Daddy was more rewarding, because now it felt like he was coming to my town. I wasn't just following him to shows anymore. He came to me and we talked about the people I'd met and who he trusted and who he didn't. On those occasions, I also got more attention from folks in the industry, because they knew I was his daughter. Daddy introduced me to so many entertainers, and that helped open doors for me.

By him being so famous, that helped me get my name around the town. I was able to meet many entertainers when I went to see my dad in the fall of 1969, and I was right in the middle of all the action during that time. We went to the Club DeLisa on the south side and the Regal Theater. Those were larger venues, where Daddy played shows, and there often were others on the bill. DeLisa had closed for a time and Pervis re-opened it with a partner and started calling it "The Club," but everyone still knew it as Club DeLisa. With Pervis being a DJ and record label owner, all the Black entertainers wanted to play there.

During this time, I had a personal crisis—I found out I was pregnant. I sure wasn't ready for no kids, but while I tried to decide how to handle it, I ended up having a miscarriage. My emotions were a jumbled mess after that, because while I wasn't ready for a child, I also wasn't ready to lose that precious gift. I took a little time to process what had happened, and then I poured that energy into my desire for a career in entertainment. Fortunately, I was welcomed into the clubs and taken care of because my daddy asked his friends to look out for me, especially when he wasn't around. That gave me a bit of protection and freedom to do things, even though I was not quite eighteen yet.

Just before my birthday, I was at the club one night with an MC named Carl Wright. He was very laid back, very cool, and very funny. He was often the comedian who would loosen up the crowd and introduce the main act. He was Pervis Spann's right-hand man, which meant he was smack dab in the middle of the music scene. He was also very protective of me. If a singer was on the show and he tried to hit on me, Carl warned him to back off. Carl had a girlfriend named Barbara West, who was an exotic dancer under the name Miss Popcorn. He introduced us and told me what she did.

She looked at me and asked, "Have you ever danced before? You look like you could be a wonderful dancer with that face and body."

I was taken by surprise, but I had learned not to let opportunity slip through my fingers. "No, but when I was young, I used to make money dancing in juke joints. I think maybe I could be a dancer if someone gave me that chance." I smiled.

So did she.

Barbara was the manager of all the dancers at a club called Mother's Lounge, over near 70th Place and Racine on the south side. Back then, Mother's Lounge was kind of new and building its reputation as a place for naughty entertainment, where comedians could talk up a blue streak while beautiful dancers in g-strings undulated nearby. Folks from the suburbs came in for dinner, a few drinks, and to watch performers late into the night.

Barbara took care of hiring and overseeing all of the dancers for the owner of the club. She told Carl that they would like to audition me for a job. He informed her that in order to do that they needed to talk to Mr. King. Carl said if he was fine with it, then they could ask me officially. "Let's get an answer from him first."

Carl told me about this and I was excited. I was young and ready to be a part of the nightlife that I had been experiencing. About two weeks later, Dad was coming to perform at The Club. I was so nervous because, at the time, he was very protective of me. He knew I had been a timid child and I usually let things bother me, so he thought the business might not be right for me. I wasn't as tough as some of the others. I guess I didn't have that edge that a lot of the more streetwise people did. When he came to town, Carl introduced him to Barbara and told him about the audition, but only if he was okay with it.

My dad told me later that he liked that people respected him enough to ask first. He looked at me and said, "Well, honey you know this is a business, right? If you take this job, you have to treat it like a business. You'll be an entertainer. Sometimes we don't get to have a life like others and our relationships are hard to keep. Everything is about show business and you need to consider this. Your boyfriend won't be happy with it and it will probably cause trouble." He was very fatherly with his advice and always protective of women, so he stressed that I needed to consider this seriously.

I said, "Dad, I would really love to do it. I think I can because when I was growing up I loved to dance and I would make a lot of money when I stayed with mom. I think this is something I could do."

"Well, if you feel that way and you understand what the life is about, I'm going to ask you to make me two promises. If you make those and keep them, I will support your decision 100 percent."

I thought, *Oh my god, if I promise him I have to keep it.* I had learned from him that your word is your bond, and if you don't tell the truth, then your word don't mean anything, so you don't have much.

I said, "Okay, Dad, what are the things I need to do in order to do this?"

"Number one, you got to promise me that you will not mess around with drugs. Number two, there are a lot of pimps out here, you know. It's part of this business."

I knew what he was talking about. It was normal for all kinds of business transactions to take place, especially around these underground-type places. I'd seen those nice-dressed men surrounded by women. A lot of them were friends with daddy and even provided him with some of his fancy clothes and probably women, for all I knew.

"Don't get involved with those guys!" he warned.

Those things made sense to me, because either one could have hurt me and my reputation, which would affect my career. So, I agreed to the "no pimps and no drugs" deal. That was an easy promise to him, and he knew I would keep it. Any time there was a tough situation like that, I would remember those words.

With that permission out of the way, I was asked to come down to the club on Thanksgiving weekend to watch the other girls and see if I thought it was something I could do.

I went down there and, sure enough, the pimps were knee deep up in there. It felt like a big trap because that was one of the two things to avoid, and drugs were there, too. Some pimps were nice and looked sharp, but I had to keep my promise. I sat and watched as the girls danced and worked the eager crowd.

The dancing hall in the back was where the men hung out and put a dollar or two in your outfit. That meant the girls really had to hustle to make any money. I was thinking, *I don't know if I can handle this.* My love for dancing outweighed the mixed feelings I was having, so I sat there imaging myself dancing on stage and making some of that cash. I would finally be a professional making a living and supporting myself doing what I'd always loved to do. It was a dream come true for a young girl like me.

The last week of December, they asked me to come back for an official audition. I had been thinking about it since I'd seen what goes on there. I was conflicted because I didn't want to be involved with some of those seedy characters, but I did want to dance, and if I did that, I had to be alluring and very sexual. Still, I looked at it as an opportunity and a stepping stone to something bigger.

I practiced in front of a mirror and experimented with moves and poses, trying to get more comfortable with the idea of being on stage half-dressed. I set my mind into audition mode and got to work on a costume. I took my best pair of panties and my nicest bra and glued some fringe on them. Then I slipped on my new go-go boots to complete the look. I was playing the part of a dancer and creating a character. It was working for me, because I was able to think about it as playing a part.

I went over to the club at the agreed upon time and went into character. I did my best dancing in my cute little outfit, wiggling and shaking my way around the stage. When I was done, they were very encouraging. They loved the way I moved and worked the audience, but there was one thing they did not like—my amateur outfit. They said my clothes were still kind of country and plain.

I didn't have any real fancy dancing outfits. The other girls were, of course, very sexy with professional-looking clothes, and my homemade fringe just wouldn't do. I was used to being more of a reserved, church type girl, so this culture was very different for me. However, they kept going on about how they loved my body and the way I moved. They also added that I needed to jack up the sexual aspect a little bit. I understood what they were saying, because those professional dancers were very alluring, and that was not me at all.

Even with those reservations, they decided to hire me and told me it was on a trial basis. I would need to step up my game, but they were willing to give me a shot in front of a real crowd. I was so excited to have a professional job in entertainment. Plus, I'd be able to earn my own money. I wouldn't need Daddy's help. I was growing up. When I told Daddy the good news, he smiled real big and congratulated me. "If you're happy, I'm happy," he said.

My boyfriend at that time gave me some protection from the horny men at the club, but I found out later that he had gotten into the game himself and was a little bit of a small-town pimp. That's what Daddy had warned me about. It was hard to tell who was and who wasn't. Most guys stayed off me because the other pimps respected his territory, but at the time I didn't realize that's why they were staying away.

Regardless of that, the dancing was fun and exciting. I really got into it. Somehow it all came together. When I wasn't dancing, I still went to the club and hung out with the entertainers playing that night. I was totally into the show business lifestyle, either dancing and entertaining or going out to shows and meeting folks. It made me very happy and I felt like I really belonged. Most nights, after the shows, that's where we had the real fun. All of the entertainers gathered at a local spot, such as Guys and Gals, and just stayed up all night talking and laughing. It was good for a career to be able to mingle with this crowd and hang with them through the night—the later, the better.

As far as the rest of my friends and family went, word spread real quickly that little Shirley was making her money dancing around on stage. They were very surprised, because I wasn't real outgoing as a child. Most folks, like my friend Barbara and her cousin Larry, were very supportive. Mrs. Johnson didn't know, but the kids in the family did and they were blown away. Oddly enough, I had moved in with them for a while until I got enough money together for a new place. It was so convenient because they lived right across the street from the Guys and Gals Club. Even before I was dancing there, we could see the action going on every night. Stars such as The Jackson 5, Patti LaBelle, and James Brown played there as they were coming up.

Watching those entertainers on stage was intoxicating for me. I just love the way James Brown owned that stage. He commanded attention from the moment he started and the audience was on their feet the whole time. He was exciting to watch. Patti LaBelle was singing solo after her group had recently broken up. She was more of a vocalist, but I loved the control of her voice and her beautiful stage clothes. I tried to learn as much as I could from all the acts that passed through. I was like a sponge—a scantily-clad sponge.

Almost every night of the week, there was an act playing at Mother's. The show usually started with a comedian, then an opening act, and then the main talent. Throughout the show, the dancers performed to entertain the crowd. Then, in between acts, the dancers took center stage.

It was exciting meeting all the up-and-coming acts. One night, The Jackson 5 were playing and I was backstage in the dressing room getting ready. I felt someone's eyes on me and found Michael Jackson spying on me through a keyhole as I got into my costume. Things often got crazy backstage and even crazier out in the club, but I loved the excitement and energy. I had found a place where I belonged and I was good at what I did.

After I had danced there for a while, I gained a reputation as one of the best dancers in the city. Word spread real fast that there was a hot new dancer in town called Shirley King, the Body Queen. It wasn't long before my name was on the sign outside letting everyone know when I would be dancing. Tickets would sell out fast and shows grew to standing room only.

One night, Barbara Johnson and a bunch of her family decided to surprise me and come to the club. Not only that, they bought a ticket for Mrs. Johnson, too, but didn't tell her that not only was I in the show, but I was also the featured dancer.

That wasn't the smartest move, I guess, because the next day Mrs. Johnson asked me to move out. She said there were young children in the home and she didn't want them to get any ideas. Barbara told me they would ask every day, "When is Shirley coming back?" Her mother always said, "She'll be back," but I never did live there again. I didn't need to.

Barbara told me her whole family—even her mother—was actually very excited by my success. She said she always thought of me as a movie star when she was little and now everyone in town was talking about me. I had learned from my dad to dress nice and project a professional image, and that's what I did. Barbara said they all used to talk about how Book should have married me when he had the chance, but I guess things go a certain way for a reason.

I never forgot the hurt and pain he had caused me, but enjoying some success and having people talk about Shirley King sure did feel good.

Shirley's stepfather, Curtis Lee Gilmer, Vincent, AK, 1963.

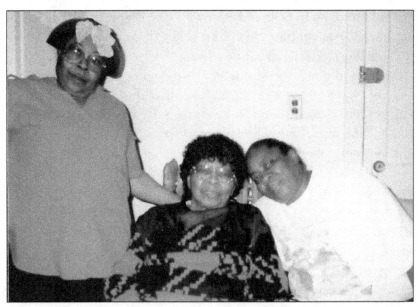

Aunt Mamie Louise, Grandma Mary, Mary Elizabeth (Shirley's mother).

Shirley's daughter, Venus, and her son, Patrick, in Chicago, 1984.

Model photo, age 19.

Another model photo.

Newspaper clipping of Shirley's early dancing career in Chicago.

Singing at a festival in Chicago, 1988.

Early singing gig, 1998.

Shirley in front of B. B. King's bus, Big Red.

Shirley and band member/dancer Malik.

Shirley and Patrick when he was working for his grandfather, B. B. King, 2006.

Shirley and her father, B. B. King, 1999.

Shirley and B.B. on his bus.

Shirley bonding with her father.

Manager Phil Stark with B. B. King.

MS, SHIRLEY A. PETERSON
Hello, How is my Beautiful Daughter? Fine I hope, I am thinking of you, I hope you are doing well, and every thing is good for You, I am really missing you! Wishing that I could see you, it's been a while, thanks for the cards, and letters, very sweet, and kind of You, I keep hearing, good things about You, You are getting there, keep it up pretty girl, today I am in Germany, I just left England, now I am in Athens, Greece, it is very hot here, reminds me of Las Vegas, it would be a nice place, to sight see, if I had the time, but I am only here one night, I guess this is all for now, remember all ways, Your Dad, is proud of You, and loves You, very much, give my love to the children,
           WITH LOVE
           YOUR DAD
           RILEY B. KING SR.

Letter from B.B. to Shirley.

Isn't it wonderful
that as time goes by
we become more and more aware
of what's really important in life?
Every Christmas we see more clearly
and know more surely
that the love our family shares
is a treasure greater
than any of the gifts
under the tree.

It's the memories
that belong to us alone,
the dreams we've shared,
the laughter and the tears,
the partings and the glad reunions,
the love that will always deepen--
These are the things
that mean the most--
at Christmas and always.

Merry Christmas
Dad
Riley B. King

Christmas card to Shirley from her father.

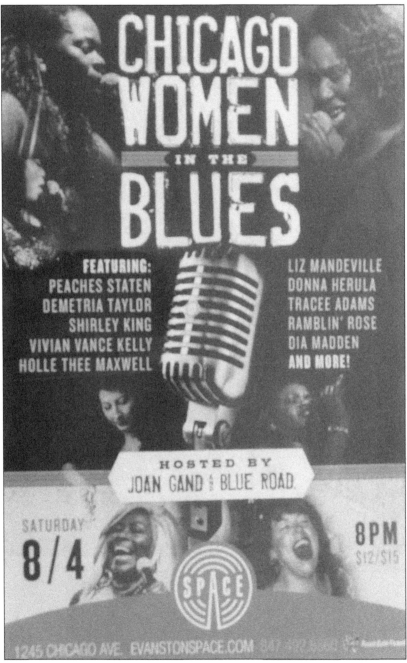

Chicago Women in the blues poster.

Shirley at The Joynt with Joe Jackson in Chicago, 2007.

Shirley at music festival with Issac Hayes, 2006.

Shirley at the Women's Blues Festival in Chicago. Courtesy of Moe Taib.

Argentina concert poster.

Shirley today. Courtesy of Dave Smitherman.

CHAPTER 6 - LOVE COMES TO TOWN

The early 1970s was an exciting time for Chicago Blues and other types of music, especially among the Black audiences that packed the nightclubs that had started popping up to handle the increased demand. Some folks that I'd seen perform many times had finally started to break through to a wider audience, such as Jackie Wilson, The Dells, and The Chi-Lites, who had big hits with "Have You Seen Her" and "Oh Girl." Everyone famous hung out at The Club. They eventually started putting on a weekly talent show, and anyone could sign up. The winner would perform for the owners, Rodney Jones and Pervis Spann, so that was a big incentive right there. They could make your music career if they wanted to.

My boyfriend at the time needed to go to The Club that night to meet up with someone, so I went along with him. It was a big night, because The Jackson Five were there to compete, too. They were working hard to build on their reputation, which had started to pick up steam. Their father, Joe Jackson, got off work at the steel mill in Indiana, loaded those boys in their car, and drove to gigs all over the area trying to get them exposed to the people in the business. He wanted Pervis to help manage them, so they played Chicago often.

Their career was on the upswing, and that meant an especially big crowd had turned out that night. For some reason, my boyfriend got it in his head that I should perform in the show, but I was shy. When I was dancing, I got lost in another world and I was able to create that character, but I didn't know what I would do as a singer. I wasn't sure that I could do it. He talked me into signing up, and after I did, I realized that the Jacksons and so many other talented people were there. I thought, *Oh god, everyone is here to see them, not me.* I wanted to take my name off the list. I was never big at competing with others. I liked to do things myself, and didn't feel comfortable having someone pick one over the others based on one performance.

They wouldn't let me out of the show, so I just gave up and said, "Fine, I'll do it." When my name was called, I went up. I was wearing another one of my homemade outfits. This was an old swimsuit that I had fashioned into a dress. It was short and sexy, and my makeup was on point. My boyfriend said I was "looking cute," so that helped with my confidence. Then, I had to pick something to sing.

I knew a wonderful singer named Betty Everett, and she had a song called "They'll Come a Time." It's a real sad tune about how everyone has to cry sometime. It's a very emotional song, and I loved it. I sang it all the time when I was alone. So, that's the song I chose. I knew it wasn't an easy, upbeat jam that would get the crowd going, but I had always thought I could put my own spin on it, and that's exactly what I did.

I got my nerve up, and when they called my name, I made my way to the stage with as much confidence and professionalism as I could muster. If I was going to do this, I was going to give it my best shot, especially with the crowd that was there that night. As the music began, I closed my eyes, waited for my cue, and started in just as I'd done in front of the mirror at home. Something magical happened in those first few seconds. I could feel the words pouring out of me like an emotional release. All of the hurt from Book, the harassment of unwanted advances from men, the absence of my father—all of that took over my soul. I bundled all of those emotions up and channeled them into the song, letting it drift out over the audience. When I opened my eyes mid-song, I was amazed by the reaction. From my viewpoint, I could see the smiling faces watching my every move, heads nodding and bodies swaying. They seemed hypnotized by what I was doing on stage. It was the most amazing feeling. I wasn't dancing and using my body as I usually did. I was just straight-up singing.

When the contest was over and they prepared to announce the winner, I was ready to go home. I had accomplished more than I'd ever expected that night. I honestly didn't care about the outcome. Before we could say our goodbyes, they made the announcement that I had won. At first I wasn't sure what had happened. *How had I won over everyone else?* I didn't like the idea of competing, but winning did plant the seed that maybe I could do something besides dancing. Don't get me wrong, though, because I loved moving my body. I was young, and dancing made me feel alive. It was just very exciting to be recognized for something . . . more.

Everyone was congratulating me. Harold Melvin and the Blue Notes were there since they had done a performance at another venue. I met a new singer named Teddy Pendergrass and was amazed by his voice. The Dells were there, The Chi-Lites were there. Garland Green, a cat who had a hit called "Jealous Kind of Fella," was there. It was just a lot of people hanging out. It was amazing, but stressful. I didn't want to do that again!

Right after I won, I was filled with adrenaline. We were at the Beale Street Club, and there were a couple of others in walking distance, so a few of us headed over to another joint. I saw more exciting entertainers. An all-girl group called Barbara and the Uniques were there. They had a hit with "There It Goes Again" written by a member of The Chi-Lites. They were trying to break through nationwide. There were a couple of male groups in the house. Ruby Andrews had a big hit with "Casanova (Your Playing Days Are Over)" and was talking about finding her next song. Sunday Williams was trying to take her big song, "Ain't Got No Problem," to the next level. It was like that everywhere in town. There was so much talent, and I took notice of the women getting into the game. Most were still at the local level, but they were doing their thing, and I liked seeing that.

As far as my dancing career, I was ready to make a change. I was always out meeting new people and making connections and felt it was time for a move. My goal was to be a "real" dancer and not just a go-go girl at a club on the south side.

I left Guys and Gals and started to look for work at Beale Street. I got a break at one of the clubs, when they offered to let me dance in the show that night. At that time, there was a man called Bill Cody, and he was in charge of creating choreography for the girls in the show. When I saw what they were doing, it was amazing. They were out of sight. It was very professional and polished, and that's what I wanted for my career. I wasn't sure if I could do it, but I wanted to try.

In the show that night were many of the regulars—Barbara and the Uniques, The Five Wages, The Deltas—they were amazing to watch. I saw how the dancers not only complemented the performances, but actually elevated them with beautiful routines. As always, I was determined to find the person in charge and introduce myself. It was all about "see and be seen" if you wanted to gain respect and credibility. I found the manager, Valerie, and talked to her. She had heard of me and knew Daddy, so that went well.

The respect Daddy had earned over the years was good for me because it helped people take notice of what I was doing and it forced me to work hard to earn that same reputation. I took my cues from him and saw how I was supposed to conduct myself to build a career. That dancing I had been doing, while avoiding pimps and handsy customers, had helped me build a nice following, and now I was ready to take it to another level. I was determined to become the best dancer in town, but remembering Daddy's advice, I decided to be smart.

I started dancing in this review show, but I still kept my gigs at Mother's Lounge to help build my fan base by performing in different parts of town. It was a hectic schedule that started with Mother's Lounge, moving on to Guys and Gals, and some late night dancing at Beale Street. I was still dating Michael while my career was exploding. I was soon known as the most interesting, exciting dancer in Chicago.

Larry Washington, Barbara Johnson's cousin, was someone I knew from back in Arkansas. In fact, I used to go over to his grandmother's house and use their phone to call Booker when he was in Chicago without me. They'd always remind me not to talk too much because it was long distance. Larry was younger than me and had recently relocated to Chicago, too. He was living with the Johnsons, and I was so excited when I saw him out in the clubs. He was very excited for me and my success.

"You are doing what you've always wanted to do and you look happy!"

"It's so good to see someone from back home," I told him.

"Look at you making money and entertainment people. It's so exciting."

It was very validating to get such a reaction from someone who hadn't seen me for a minute. That made me feel good, and we developed such a deep friendship. We would have so much fun cutting up in the clubs.

One night, I was dancing, and Larry was in the audience being supportive as usual. He yelled, "Shirley, hold that position!" and he ran off to the bathroom.

I had to give the audience what they wanted, so I stopped dancing and just held the awkward pose, peeking to the side with one eye to see when he was coming back. Finally he did.

"You held it all that time?"

"Just for you, Larry."

Through the early 1970s, the music scene evolved like it always does. Clubs came and went, changed management, and varied in popularity depending on word in the street. Pervis had grown his business and was bringing in more famous acts. Club DeLisa became The Burning Spear and was soon the hot spot again. Daddy even started playing there when he was in town.

They had a hot new comedian named Wilbur "Hi-Fi" White. He was over the top, and everyone loved and respected him. (He was also a singer and later acted on TV and in movies.) He had been around for a while developing his act and he was good friends with Redd Foxx. With the shows that were put on, a comedian could make or break a club with his reputation since he often set the tone for the night. Hi-Fi was different from most. He was funny and flirty, and not just with the women; he teased the men, too, but he was very playful and not at all intimidating. Everyone took it in stride, and I was intrigued by this different type of performer.

One night, I was down at the club after working at Mother's Lounge and Carl Wright and his girlfriend were there. They had a new singer who was performing that night. I had just recently seen Teddy Pendergrass and didn't think anyone could top him, but when I saw this new guy singing about being alone, those words were comfort to my soul. At the end of the night after the show was over, Carl told me this guy wanted to meet me.

"You know I got a boyfriend," I said. "I don't like him like that. I just liked that song."

Carl said, "Why don't you just meet the guy?"

"Okay."

The dressing rooms were all downstairs, so that's where the performers went at the end of the show. He introduced me to this new talent.

"Shirley, this is Al Green."

I said "Al Green? Okay, hi."

We started talking and I wasn't interested in him that way because I was in love with the man I was with. I wanted to be straight up with him from the jump because I don't like misunderstandings. I told him that I have a friend, and even though he was dealing with other females, he had recently given me a car. We had broken up, but were trying to work things out. I was in love, so I stayed with him. He would come over whenever he got ready. Love does these things. Love has you blind, but I was very clear that I was not looking for a boyfriend.

Al said, "I don't want to be your boyfriend. Can't we just get together and talk?"

I said, "No, that wouldn't look right."

"Okay."

I had to be careful with my shows and my money as an entertainer. There were some real shady characters in the Chicago club scene. Come to find out, the promoters that had booked Al's show had up and left with all the money. Al didn't get a penny. That meant he was stranded. Al was living in Michigan and had to call his girlfriend to have her wire him some money so he could get back home.

I saw this play out in front of me.

"When will your money get here?" I asked.

He said he just needed somewhere to wait until it came through. I trusted him and wasn't worried. I was used to helping folks in the business. That's what we did, lend a hand when someone needed it. I allowed him to stay at my place that night. He talked a lot and tried to make it clear he was attracted to me, but maybe because of who my daddy was, he didn't try anything. He slept on the couch and his money came in the morning.

Things with my man had gone from bad to worse. He was clearly not a one-woman man. I couldn't understand it, and we fought a lot. Half the time, I wanted to be with him, but he was often out on the town and I couldn't locate him. I didn't like to be involved with more than one man on the sexual tip. There was not enough room in my feelings for two men. I stayed and we continued to fight, break up, and reconcile. This went on for about five years.

As we continued to work on our relationship, I went with my boyfriend to Mississippi to see his grandparents. They made us sleep in different rooms, which was fine, but what was not fine was that my boyfriend went out and left me there. I was stuck out in the country night after night, alone with his grandparents. I finally got a ride to a pay phone and I called Al. He had given me his number and said that since I'd helped him, I could call if I needed something.

When he answered, I told him, "I need to get home and I don't have any money or a way to get out. I am stranded."

He said, "Where are you?"

"I'm down here in Mississippi."

"How far is the Greyhound bus station?"

"It's a ways off, but I can probably get a ride."

"I will buy you a ticket and if you can get there, it will take you to Memphis. Then, I'll make sure you can get to Chicago. You were a very good friend to me when I needed one, and now it's my turn."

That made me smile.

He added, "So go get on that bus!"

It was good to hear someone laugh again. When I finally got ahold of my boyfriend, I told him that I couldn't take it anymore and needed to get to the bus station. After a little back and forth, he finally agreed and took me. Just as promised, there was a ticket waiting for me from "Albert." That's my grandfather's name, so I thought maybe it was a sign of good things to come.

When I got to Memphis, there was Al sitting in the bus station. He had on some short pants and a crazy-looking top, and beside him was a huge dog. I wasn't so excited about the dog, but I thought maybe he could take me across the bridge to Arkansas so I could stay with my mom until I figured out how to get back to Chicago. We got in the car and he was happy to see me and said he hoped we could be friends. He said he was working with Willie Mitchell on a new record. He made me feel like he cared. Anytime I got that feeling from a man and I was single, I would go into love mode and . . . that's what happened.

He had been there when I needed him, and becoming part of his life was amazing. He was so romantic. We sometimes got in his car and took late night rides looking at beautiful homes and dreaming about a future together. We went to nice restaurants and had expensive dinners, lingering at the table until way past closing time. I had never experienced anything like that. It was heavenly. I didn't know men like him existed. The fact that he was also an entertainer was even better. He was in demand, but chose to spend his time with me. I felt way past special.

I was going to stay for a couple of days, but that turned into a week and then a month. I didn't want it to end. We did things I'd only seen in movies. He was so charming, attentive, and passionate. He moved my mind to another level. In my other relationships, the man had never been so focused on me and my needs. It made me feel so special that, at first, it was actually unsettling. I'd never had someone so concerned about my feelings, and it felt amazing. Every time I was supposed to leave, I found an excuse to stay, or he found one. I wanted to stay there forever, but I knew I had a career and commitments back in Chicago. When I actually had to leave for real, my eyes were dripping with tears.

I had always wanted to be loved so hard and deep. I thought I'd finally gotten it right. I had called my mom and told her who I was with. He was very big in the South and was getting more popular by the minute.

I told Al about her. He said, "Let's go see your mom."

We stopped along the way and he bought some food to take as a gift. My family went crazy because the famous Al Green was right there. They loved it. When he gave them the food, they were just so excited. They wanted autographs and made plans to come to his next show. Mama cooked soul food for him and, as always, her meals were delicious. It was such a happy family time. *Is this man going to be my husband?* I wondered.

We went back to Memphis and had to face reality. I had to get back to work, and he was going on tour.

I said, "I'd like to come back and visit."

He said, "I told you I was going to get you, didn't I?"

I got concerned when he said that because I thought maybe it was a challenge for him, but he assured me it wasn't. He even sang a few of his new songs for me. Some of them were so romantic, and he told me I was the inspiration.

Finally, he took me to the bus station. I cried from Memphis all the way to Chicago. I'd finally met my best friend and then I had to leave. When I got back, the boyfriend had returned from Mississippi and he never asked me why it took so long for me to return. He never spoke of it and pretended everything was fine. It was never the same after that month with Al. He taught me how I should be treated by a man.

By 1973, I was dancing at the Road Runner Lounge on route 75, way over on the east side. In addition, I was doing shows at Beale Street and still at Mother's Lounge. My name had gotten around as the city's premier dancer. My absence even helped fuel the demand for my services.

I did notice, though, that the club scene was changing with this new sound called Disco music. One night, I was dancing at the Road Runner and the promoter brought in a group of female impersonators and drag queens who put on lip sync shows, where they pretended they were singing to someone else's recording. I'd never seen anything like it, and they were pretty amazing. It was something new that was spreading through the club scene. It was very flamboyant, and they could often interpret the song better than the original artist. It was a very visual performance.

That night, there were four impersonators and Michael Peterson, a guy who could actually sing Aretha Franklin songs. He wasn't in a costume like the others, but he sounded just like Aretha. He was a handsome, well-dressed man, and when he sang in her voice, he surprised me. It blew my mind. I was so overwhelmed by anyone who had real, undeniable talent. When I heard him I thought, *Wow! I could make some money with him.* My business side kicked in. I could build my own show with him singing and me dancing. After he finished singing, I noticed that he kept staring at me. I didn't know why because I just assumed he was gay since he was running with these folks. That was the concept of the show, right?

I had gotten pretty good at turning down men without hurting their ego and I definitely didn't want to offend him because we might be able to make money together. So, we started talking and my fears were quickly put aside. We became fast friends and we started hanging out after our shows. We talked about our relationships and the experiences we'd had in this business.

One night, I suggested to Michael that I would like to book him on some shows with me. He said he would love it. So, the last time I was at the Road Runner, I was out there dancing and I could see him in the backstage dressing room with the door open. He was staring at me. I got the feeling he was interested in me, and that just was not something I had anticipated.

After our performance, we stuck to tradition and everyone went to a diner or after-hours club and talked until five o'clock or six o'clock in the morning. We went home and slept all day. That was our routine. Wake up at nine at night, perform, socialize, and then fall asleep as the sun came up. When I took him home, he didn't want to get out of the car. We kept talking. I knew we didn't have anything in common sexually because we both liked men, but I did enjoy his friendship very much.

One morning, Michael invited me into his house to meet his family. I thought, *That's cute. He wants me to meet his family, to be a part of his life. I like that.* I went in and met them and everyone was very nice. He had three sisters, his mother, and him. *No wonder he sings like Aretha, he's just around girls.*

He had a room downstairs since he was the only man in the house. He asked if I wanted to see it. He had a white rabbit that was nibbling on everything. I tried to be fond of the rabbit, just to be nice to him. The sisters admired him and had him sing at all their parties. He was the show person of the family. As we kept talking, I realized how much we had in common. We were the showoffs in our families, both in entertainment and both looking for something more. The manly side of him seemed to come out when we were alone. He started telling me how he had been touched a few times by the minister at his church. I don't know what all happened, but I was very sympathetic and started seeing him as a man who wanted to be a man if he met the right woman . . . me.

We decided it was time to start our own revue. The first night, I had booked us at a place where we could perform a run-through of our showcase. We billed Michael as "Mr. Aretha Franklin." We brought his three sisters to perform backup, but when they got there, stage fright took over and they chickened out. They wouldn't go on stage and perform like we had rehearsed. I couldn't believe it. They had seemed so confident during rehearsal. The club owner was not happy.

"What am I going to do? You said you'd put on a show here and I advertised it that way."

We said, "Okay, we will do the show!"

Michael did his Aretha thing and blew the roof off the place. The audience was amazed. Then, I went and did my dance routine.

Later, we were sitting in the corner talking and the boyfriend that I had been dealing with previously was supposed to meet me at the club to give me a ride home. It was no surprise that he never showed up.

Michael said, "Man, he don't appreciate you. He don't know what he got. If I was your man, I wouldn't treat you like that."

I said, "If you was my man?" I thought of him like a good girlfriend of mine. Then, he started saying the things that I felt like my boyfriend should be saying.

On the way home, he started talking about how much he cared about me and how he had liked me for a long time. Somehow, someway, it just felt right. I'm still not real sure how it happened like that.

The next morning, things seemed real good, and I thought to myself, *Maybe this was the answer to my relationship troubles. Here's somebody who wants and needs me.* We talked about getting together. When he told his family that I was now his girlfriend, they looked at each other in surprise. I guess everyone was puzzled. I was just so happy for someone wanting me. I felt like I had someone who loved me, plus he was talented and very handsome. The complete package.

A couple of days later, Michael proposed. My mind was blown. I was totally confused. Being together was one thing, but marriage? I couldn't figure out how it had happened, but I did feel happy. There was no denying that. He wanted to get married in October, and my birthday is October 26, so we decided on October 22, 1973 as our wedding date.

He didn't waste any time. In August, he had proposed, and by October, we were at City Hall getting the paperwork and saying "I do" in front of a judge. We walked out husband and wife. My name was no longer Shirley Ann King; now I was Shirley Ann King Petersen.

I felt like everything had moved way too fast, but it did feel good to be wanted so much. He insisted on a life with me. When we walked out of the courthouse, he said, "Now if any man even looks at you I have the right to kick his butt."

I thought, *What? Being a dancer, people flirting with me is part of the job, and this could ruin the career I had worked so hard for.* I didn't need a jealous man coming between me and my money.

About five months after that, Al Green had a hit called "Back Up Train" and then "I'm So Tired of Being Alone" He was getting famous like he had always wanted. I hadn't talked to him much, but I saw him whenever he came to town.

He came into Chicago one time and was playing at the High Chaparral. I had told him I wasn't interested in anything physical, but I still, of course, thought about him anytime I heard him on the radio. I was now committed to another man. I was in a fix. I wasn't sure what to do. I didn't tell Al that I had gotten married. I figured, *We had fun, but it was over, so there was no need to tell him about it.* He used to ask me to fly to his shows, and at first I did, but now was a new time.

When Al finally did come to Chicago before I was married, he called me, and we usually hooked up. This time, he called my house and Michael answered. After the call, he snapped because he already felt intimidated that Al and I had been involved. I don't know what he said, but when I got home he told me, "Your boy-friend called, but I told him not to call here no more."

When I later tried to explain things to Al, he said, "You could have gotten me killed. I don't want to be around you now that you are married."

I was hurt because that's not the way I wanted that to end.

Michael and I teamed up with our act and, just as I had thought, we were a hit—I mean we were making a killing! We made money at night, and he even had a day job, so we were doing well. Things were looking good for us.

I found out that people on the street were teasing Al Green that he had lost his girlfriend to another girl, making fun of my husband. I didn't like that, but we were doing so well that I didn't pay that no mind.

However, I did notice a change in Michael. He became very possessive and called me fifteen times a day. It made me feel so trapped that I started regretting my decision to marry him. I had a friend, and she and her brother hung out with us, and both of them were infatuated with my husband. It was an odd, crazy situation. That life and those people started draining me. I felt like I had to protect myself from everyone. My world became confusing. I wasn't sure what I had gotten into, but thank God we didn't have kids together.

One day, we went to the mall at 95th and Western. It was the place to hang out where everyone went to shop and see friends. While we were there, Michael snapped again about something and he was cussing me out at the mall. I was fighting with him, and he took my keys. I had to call my previous boyfriend for help because I was stuck. He actually showed up and took me home. I finally had to call Michael's family and ask them to try and calm him down, but they didn't want to get involved. I was miserable. I felt I had married him to make my previous boyfriend jealous. It was not the right thing to do since I was not really in love with him. I realized that now.

Eventually, Michael moved back with his family because things were not working out between us. He was very angry most of the time. Then, I found out he was just like his father, who had also been very violent. They both had the demon inside and it felt like they just had "female hate." I always was told by Daddy that a man who loves his mother will love you the same, but a man that has no respect for his mother and don't love his mother is not a good guy. This guy really had self-hate. At the time, I didn't understand what was happening.

A pattern had developed. He was living at home, yet he came over and said he was sorry. I felt bad, so we got back together, but then we fought again—happened over and over for a year.

I was good friends with my previous boyfriend's brother, and told him I wanted to travel and get away from this situation. I had a brand-new car and I wanted to get in that car and hit the road. Wherever the wind took me was where I wanted to go.

We took off on a cross-country adventure. He was acting as my chauffeur, just the two of us. He was like my real brother. We were young and looking for an escape. As we hit a new town, I tried to dance somewhere if I could to make a little folding money to get us to the next state. If my dad was playing nearby, I saw him, enjoyed his show, and kept on traveling. We drove until we ended up in Las Vegas, and then we drove on to California.

I started really enjoying life. I put the marriage and the ex-boyfriend behind me. Because I was traveling with his brother, I felt like I was still connected to him in some small way. We just had fun and got really tight on a friendship level. Things didn't seem as bad anymore. I felt better about my life. I was finally carefree again. That lasted for about five months.

When I returned to Chicago, Michael tried to reconcile with me, but I didn't want to deal with that no more. The ex-boyfriend started talking to me again, too. We got together, and I got pregnant. I was not ready to have a baby, so I went and had an abortion. I didn't want to bring a child into the world like that. It wasn't the right way to do it. Then, I started hearing he already had kids with other women, so it was for the best.

I started talking again to Michael, and we reconciled and decided to try again to make the marriage work. I suggested, "Why don't we get away and start fresh somewhere? How about California?" Traveling had been so good for my spirit I thought maybe it would do the same for our relationship.

Oh, how did I not know I was creating a monster? We moved to California, where there was a large gay population. I thought I was getting him away from the female impersonating scene, but it was even bigger there than it was back in Chicago. After we had other fights, he went and hung out with his new gay friends. It was not how I had envisioned our reconciliation.

While I was in a personal whirlwind, Daddy's career was going through its own kind of change, but a positive one. He was appearing on TV shows, such as *The Ed Sullivan Show* and later on *The Tonight Show* and *The Merv Griffin Show*. He knew that this would expose him to that wide audience he had been trying to reach. With television becoming such an important way to experience entertainment, Daddy had to use that to his advantage. Each time he made an appearance, it helped him and, ultimately, it helped me. The more people who knew who my dad was, the wider my recognition became. People outside of the Chicago music scene started hearing about me. It made people want to include me in their projects, because it would give added exposure by using the King name, and I was fine with that, if it was right for me.

Despite my personal troubles, I had met a man named Rudy Ray Moore. He was a very popular comedian, musician, singer, and just an all-around entertainer. Rudy was now out in California and he'd told me when we met that he liked the way I danced. He was getting ready to film another movie after his successful film, *Dolemite* (1975). He wanted to know if I would dance in it. It would take some time to put it all together, but it would be loosely based on his club routine and then have a storyline about capturing a gangster. I was excited because this was yet another layer I could add to my career. I loved dancing, but I knew I had to plan for the next phase. Being in a movie would help raise my profile even more, not just in Chicago, but across the country.

"What's the movie called?" I asked.

"*The Human Tornado.*"

Chapter 7 - The Human Tornado

By 1974, I had divorced my first husband and was married to my second. This time, I was sure that he was the one and we would build a nice little life together, but we were already having problems. I was getting ready for a show when I started feeling sick. It was a sensation I remembered from before, and it was soon confirmed by the doctor that I was pregnant. He estimated that the baby would be born in September or October. I almost fainted when I heard the news. I didn't want to get another abortion since I'd already reluctantly done that. I cried, cried, and cried. When I was growing up, I never thought I'd want children, especially because of my situation growing up. I had seen so many families like mine where the father was not present.

If I was to have children, I wanted them to have a father around because I knew how frustrating it was not to have that. We always wanted better for our children, and I was determined to do right by mine. Despite those efforts, life got in the way and my dream of a two-parent family did not look like it would happen. Not only were my husband and I fighting and getting back together often, but I was still dancing and anything that messed with my body would not be good for my money.

I had a solid reputation around town as Shirley King, the Body Queen and I was the one everyone called when they needed a dancer. I was now incorporating more unique moves and poses into my dance style and audiences just couldn't get enough. Believe me when I tell you I threw myself into those performances. It was like I was taken over by a dancing spirit once I got into the zone of a performance.

My career momentum would certainly be affected by this pregnancy. I was thinking that not only is this going to mess with my body, but I'm pregnant by a man who I can't tolerate right now. It took everything I had inside of me to keep going. Every day, I got stronger and stronger in my decision to move forward with this child.

I met a minister, who had me in church every day, as I drew the strength to face this new chapter of my life. I had been carefree and solely focused on my career and myself up to that point. Things would be different with a child. Not only that, I didn't want my child to be embarrassed by what I did for a living. Now that I was going to be a mother, I wanted to be a good role model. Just like with my career, once I identified a goal and set my mind on it, I gave it everything I had. This baby was going to get my full attention and that meant thinking about more than just the next gig. I needed to focus on the future.

I found out that I was having a girl child and figured even though I could tell already that my marriage would not last, I could handle that. Getting into the right mindset and coming to terms with being a mother, the news about having a girl gave me something to look forward to. I relaxed in the fact that I could provide for her, and while a father is very important in a girl's life, I felt that it would be a little easier than if I was having a boy. First, I had to get my life in order and get myself together. I had to be a mother for my child, and that meant I needed to tie up some loose ends before she was born.

When I told Daddy that I was pregnant, he was very happy for me. He knew that I was married and on my own, so he liked that. He also appreciated that I was making a good living in show business just like him. I did tell him that I wasn't sure if my marriage would work out and he gave me good advice, as always. He told me to stand on my own if I needed to, just the way he had always told me. He was very generous with me (and everyone in his life) and offered to help out with my child if I needed it.

Then, I called my husband, who was now living in California. I told him that I was pregnant.

He said, "If you let me have the baby, I will raise her for you."

I said "Are you a fool? I'm not going to carry this child for nine months and go through the physical challenges just to hand her over to you. Oh, no. Of course we can share in raising her, but I won't let her be in an unsafe environment." That's where we left it.

I didn't even see him for many months, and I didn't really care. I was preparing for the birth and actually getting excited. My doctor and everyone else assured me that I'd get my shape back in no time and be able to work to support my new baby.

On October 27, 1975, my beautiful daughter, Venus, was born, just two hours after my birthday. I considered her a belated gift. Growing up I had seen many babies, but when I saw her I was almost speechless. She was just gorgeous; such a pretty baby and she even had a little shape already! She was so much like her mama.

Once I began taking care of her, things started to feel much better. I was getting into the routine of being a new mother and I poured all of my energy into that child. I was twenty-six and ready for this new life raising a baby as best I could. All of my focus went into being a good mother and making sure my daughter had the best of everything. I started buying clothes and toys right away. When she turned a year old, I even got her a complete bedroom set of her own, something I never had. I loved caring for her.

Just a few months after Venus was born, I went out to California to take care of a few things. My now ex-husband wanted to see his daughter, of course. I also wanted to show her off to the family out there. It was also time for Rudy Ray Moore to film his movie, and he still wanted me in the dance scene. I was scared because I'd just had a baby and didn't feel I was in quite the shape I'd like to be, but he said to come on out and don't worry about it.

When I got there, I met up with my first husband and we had a long talk about my situation. By this time, he was more involved in the gay lifestyle and had a partner living with him. He was still performing his Aretha songs in gay clubs. Our visit was not as smooth as I would have liked. He wanted to keep Venus for an extended period of time, but I just didn't know what his living situation was like. I didn't want her in an unstable or volatile type of environment. I didn't have a problem with how he lived his life, but I was concerned that it was not a solid foundation for her. I was in very protective mama mode.

I was out in California and not sure what my next move would be. I could have tried to continue dancing, but it wasn't as popular out there like in Chicago. I, of course, wasn't in shape like I used to be. It was a tough time for me, because my family out West had grown close to my ex and had a real connection with him. He could be very charming and he'd worked his way into their lives. So, I felt a little on the outside of my own family. It was not the welcome I had expected. Here I was with no love from my ex, none from my family, and I needed to decide my next move. I was working hard to get back into shape because I knew whatever I did, if it was in entertainment, I'd need my body to be on point.

I met up with Rudy and his girlfriend, and they were very supportive.

"I need you in my movie, Shirley," he told me.

"Rudy, I'd love to do that, but I just had my baby. I ain't ready for no close-up!"

He was determined. "You will be amazing."

I will say it did feel good to have someone so sure of me and my talent. I had people in my corner and that helped give me confidence. I was moving around a lot and staying in hotels. I wasn't sure where I would be, but I kept my daughter with me at all times. At one of the hotels, I met a very nice woman and we became friends. Come to find out she was a prostitute, and several others lived there, as well. This was one of those long-term-stay hotels. It turned out that they were the most supportive group of women I could have encountered. They came in my life when I needed it and became a great support system. They loved Venus and helped with her and even brought me baby supplies. It was an unusual situation, but I was learning that family is much more than your blood kin. They are the people who stand by you when things get tough.

When it came time to film the movie, I found out that, as promised, I was the dancer in a nightclub scene just like what happened during a lot of the shows in Chicago. I'd dance and dazzle the audience during the monologue and the intermissions as the band played on. I had on a gold bikini with fringe that I could shake around. I had gotten into pretty good shape, but still felt a little self-conscious about my stomach so they painted gold glitter on it. Everyone assured me that my curves looked great and that was all I needed to hear.

In no time I was back in the dancer zone. As the music played and Rudy did his thing, I started moving and shaking like I had rehearsed. I was determined to give it all I had for the movie. It was exciting to be in the middle of the cameras and lights which just helped to feed into my energy.

They told me that I'd be cut into the scenes "so just keep dancing and doing your thing." *Well, all right, I can do that.* So, I shook that fringe like crazy. After several moves around the stage, I dropped into a split, put my hands over my head and pulsed my legs, making my butt shake and bounce to the music. Then, in one swift move, I laid on my back, raised my butt up in the air, grabbed my ankles, and slid across the floor, bouncing and popping my chest as I inched along. The "audience" and crew went crazy and it felt good to be back in the game.

After filming, I wasn't sure where I would land. I figured, *If I could get back to Chicago, things will fall into place . . . somehow.* I needed to get some money together because being out West and not working regularly, and taking care of a little baby, meant I was low on funds.

One night, I went out to a club to observe and see if maybe they had some work for me. I ran into "Big Mama" Thornton's sister. Big Mama Thornton was a well-known singer. In fact, in 1952, she was the first to record "Hound Dog" years before Elvis did it in 1956. She also performed with my dad a few times.

When I introduced myself, her sister told me who she was. I told her about my situation. She shared with me how Big Mama was sick and had lost a lot of weight. We spent time together and it was nice to connect with a woman in the business. I told her I was looking for work so I could get my money together to go back to Chicago. Back then, you could buy a Greyhound bus voucher that allowed you to travel all around until it was used up. She had one that was still good and offered it to me, which I thought was so kind. I thanked God for helping me during those hard times by having good people cross my path.

I had a girlfriend, who I'd gone to school with as a child, and her husband was stationed out in California, so she told me to look them up. I went and stayed with them for a little while until I could get myself together. Living on the army base was only for immediate family, so her husband wasn't happy that us living there might jeopardize his career. I realized the time was now, so Venus and I made it to Los Angeles and boarded the Greyhound for Chicago.

The trip took me and my baby three days and two nights, but we did it. It was not easy, and when we finally arrived, I had never been so happy to see my adopted city. I wasn't sure what my next move would be, but at least I was home.

The Human Toronado came out in 1976, and it was exciting going to the premier in Chicago. I was usually very confident about performing, but I was a little nervous since I'd never seen myself on the big screen. Those nerves went away real fast when my part came on and everyone in the theater started screaming and cheering "I know her!" I was a little embarrassed to be sitting there watching myself, but it was a lot of fun and helped to elevate my name in the entertainment world. People kept congratulating me on it for weeks later.

Then, I heard that some of the guys were watching a copy of the movie in Daddy's Big Red bus and apparently they recognized me and told my dad that they saw me in the movie. Only thing is . . . I hadn't told him about it.

He called me right up. "Oh honey, why didn't you tell me you were in a movie?"

"Daddy, I was dancing and I didn't know if you would be proud of me doing that."

"Honey, you were in a major movie. If you are in a major movie, you are part of something that's big. It's an achievement. I'm very proud of you. You are such a good dancer."

It was praise from my father, but since it was about dancing and I had on a revealing outfit, I did feel somewhat embarrassed. He saw it for the entertainment value and understood that it was show business. As long as I didn't break his "no drugs, no pimps" rule, he stood by his word and supported my career, which was a real blessing.

I still had a relationship with the mother of my previous boyfriend, Manuel, and she offered to let us stay with her, so we moved into her house. I referred to her as my "play mother," and she got very attached to my daughter. Even her husband liked having a baby around. He worked all day and came home at night holding out his greasy hands looking for the baby to hold. I didn't mind, because they were helping me and they loved my daughter. That was a happy time for me. It was like a small family setting. Manuel still came over often since he was close with his mother.

During this time, I picked my old dancing gigs back up and even added new ones. Things started going so well that I had to hire other dancers to keep up with the demand. I couldn't be everywhere, but I could provide dancers that I felt would represent me well. It was rewarding to know that I was back to performing. The attention I received from the movie helped spread the word that Shirley was back. I could barely keep up, but I was happy. My play mother took care of my daughter while I was dancing and finally making good money.

The ex-boyfriend kept thinking we would get back together, and he was right. We did. Briefly. Then, I was pregnant again.

It was the worst thing that could happen because my life was back on track. I did a lot of praying and soul searching. I just could not afford to be out of work again for a long period of time. I had learned after being away that if you're not seen around town, you can easily be forgotten. It's hard to get back in, and I wasn't ready to let that go. After lots of prayer, I got another abortion in 1980.

There was a little downtime, but not much. I went back to dancing and got on birth control so I wouldn't have to do that ever again.

Later, I was dating a musician, and even while on birth control—it happened again! This time, I knew I couldn't go through ending another pregnancy, and after nine months, my son, Patrick, was born on January 13, 1981. I named him after his father, and I really tried to have a relationship with his father. He was involved at first. He seemed cool with me and my daughter and treated her like his child—until his son came into the world. Then, he had a baby by another woman, so I was ready to let him go. I didn't want to deal with more drama.

Finally, we did reconcile once again and that resulted in yet another pregnancy. I just couldn't afford to have another child, financially or mentally. I had another, last abortion. That was a total of four children that I didn't bring into the world and two that I did, and they didn't have a father present. (I've thought a lot about what all of that means and how my life would have been different if I'd had all of those children. I would have gladly done so if I had a stable home life, but that just wasn't the case. It was a struggle to raise two kids on my own. I've just learned that I have to take responsibility for my choices, make amends if I can, pray about it, and move on with my life.)

When Venus was six, she was in first grade and the big sister to Patrick, who was two. She took him to school and was very responsible. I told them, "It's the three of us against the world. The three of us stick together. Anybody want to deal with us, it's all of us." I didn't care about what other people thought, it was always me and my kids. That was my new mindset. I was no longer the carefree dancer that I'd been for so long.

With Patrick's father out of the picture, the kids learned from very early on to be self-sufficient. I was working when I could. I kept dancing for a while, but it was not the lifestyle for a young mother. I couldn't stay out late like I used to. To make ends meet, I tried a few other ways to pay the rent, like rummy and even a little betting on the ponies. I was fully immersed in my life as a mother, but I was also trying to find my way professionally. I was able to take them with me a few times when I danced, just as my mother had done long ago at the juke joints, and how I'd gone to watch Daddy perform. They waited backstage while mommy went out to perform. Then, I changed clothes and rushed them home to bed.

As my son got older, I lived in places I really couldn't afford, because I wanted them, especially my son, to be in a nice neighborhood. I wasn't totally worried about my daughter, because she was a little older, but I was concerned that my son might get in with the wrong crowd. I was a female trying to raise a boy child. That has always been tough in our culture. It's very difficult for a woman to raise a confident Black man, because we just can't provide the guidance that a father or other grown man can. We can talk and teach them, but we can't be that male example.

At some point along the way, my son thought I had more love for my daughter than I did for him. I think I said a few things that I probably shouldn't have said, and he heard that, and took it the wrong way. I remember once I did say, "When my daughter was born, she was pretty and wonderful, and when my son was born, he was different-looking." That was true, but as a single mother, I was learning that I had to be careful how I treated them.

The tables flipped at one point and my daughter was sure that my son was more important to me. It was hard because here I had two people in the world that I loved so much and both were feeling threatened by each other. Each having a different daddy probably did not help things. That meant the love we were supposed to have together was not working. It was me competing with my daughter and my son, and my son competing with me and my daughter. I guess I didn't do a lot of things right. I asked God every day to give me the wisdom to understand what I had done to mess this up. If there was any way I could have fixed it, I would have, because it wasn't my intent to have a disconnected family.

I was dating here and there, but it was difficult with trying to dance and having two young children. Seemed like every time I got hooked up with a man, he'd end up with a drinking problem or worse.

Since I was in the business, I dated a lot of musicians, especially bass players. I met a man named Malik Abdullah in the 1980s, and he was a break dancer and stripper along with his wife, Doll Baby. Since I still had my dancing thing going on, I was always looking for new talent. He worked at a local disco. Somehow we were introduced and began talking. (I found out later that he knew of my reputation around town.)

He told me that I was sort of an urban legend, this amazing dancer with the famous father. I found out there were even rumors that I was James Brown's daughter. All kinds of things were floating around. Mostly true, but with a lot of falsehoods sprinkled in. I was used to it.

When Malik Abdullah and I met, and I saw what he could do, I asked if he'd like to open for me. At some shows, I had male dancers start off the show and then come in at certain times. He was excited, because he said I was considered "classy" and "the big time." (He later told me that when he met me "it looked like someone had drawn me.")

As we started to work together, he loved it because I only worked in nice places and he was used to hustling for a gig, so this was good for him. We were paid well and made some nice money. Anyone who worked for me was able to build a reputation as performing with the top dancer in town, so it was very flattering to have so many people want to join my show.

During the 1980s, while I thought about my next professional move, Daddy was really hitting the big time. First, there was a biography of him published in 1980 called *The Arrival of B. B. King* by Charles Sawyer. It was a very well-researched book by a man who had known Daddy for a long time. I was thanked in the acknowledgements and mentioned in the book, which was very nice.

By the mid-1980s, Daddy was working with the popular band, U2, and joining them on their world tour. He also received a Lifetime Achievement Grammy in 1987, so he had officially crossed into the mainstream consciousness and it was great for his career.

He still continued to tour like crazy, even bringing a specially-made bus across the ocean all the way from Belgium so he could ride in style. He had a rule of no females traveling on the bus with him. I guess all those men would tend to get a little rowdy and wouldn't feel comfortable with ladies around. That was okay with me because he often flew me and my kids to one of his shows, and put us up in a hotel. We spent some time with him after the shows. I heard stories about how he loved watching cartoons in the back of the bus every Saturday morning. His favorite characters were the Road Runner and other Looney Tunes.

My kids were getting a little older, and I was ready for a change of pace. I had been dancing for a total of twenty-one years. By 1989, I had had enough and felt like I shouldn't be exposing myself anymore. I would usually come out in a G-string and pasties, and it was time to end that. I wanted to stop while I was on top of the dancing game. I was not ashamed of showing my body on the dance floor, after all it was just an act. Anyone who knew me outside of the clubs saw that I was much more reserved when I wasn't dancing.

Remembering my success at the talent show and how people responded to my singing, I started thinking about that as my next move. Malik and I went to the same church, and he was also looking for something more oriented toward music, so I thought maybe things could work out.

Around that time, I also met a guy named Billy Branch, a well-educated man, who loves the Blues. He was known for playing with the Willie Dixon All-Stars and eventually with lots of other folks, such as Lou Rawls, Koko Taylor, and Taj Mahal. He had three Grammy Award nominations under his belt and even lost once to my daddy and Eric Clapton!

Billy was the one who got me more involved in the Blues music scene and he encouraged me to do my own thing. He called his band The Sons of Blues, and I was later dubbed "the Daughter of the Blues" because of my father. I went to Billy's shows with Shirley Dixon (Willie Dixon's daughter) and she was singing a bit, as well. Billy let us sit in on his shows, and with each performance I became more confident in my abilities. He came into my life at just the right time and we worked well together. We were a good team. I started meeting others in the industry, such as Koko Taylor and her daughter. The late 1980s were a hot time for music in Chicago and there were a lot of folks doing well off of making music.

I remember a man named Alvin Cash. He had a record called "Twine Time." The song had a dance with it, which meant that anytime it started, Alvin became "the twine man." He ended up a one-hit wonder, but at the time he was pretty big. Everybody knew him and had loved him for "twine time." Through him, I met other famous people, because he was connected since his song was always recognized. Like Billy, he believed in me and wanted to help me. Being around these experienced musicians gave me the confidence to go out on my own. Many people helped me because either they knew of me through my dancing, they respected my dad, or both.

Around 1989, Chicago was musically exciting. There was "Record Row" from 12th Street to almost 24th Street, where lots of record companies started popping up. There were local and national labels mixed in together, and the big hangout place was Batts Restaurant, where a lot of music folk talked business over drinks. Blues was very popular at the time, as was Soul and R&B. All types of music was represented, and there were clubs such as High Chaparral, the Algiers Lounge, Guys and Gals, and Budland over on the south side. The west side had the Peppermint Lounge and the Sidewinder.

We could feel the excitement in the air. There was a lot going on and I happened to get into it at the right time. Koko Taylor, Eddie Shaw, Eddie Clearwater, Magic Slim, Lefty Dizz, Garland Green, Johnny Williams, Alvin Cash, and Bobby Jones. Oh my! The list goes on and on.

There were also popular groups, such as The Dells and The Chi-Lites playing at the clubs around town. That world belonged to me at that time. I felt like a big part of the music world. Everybody was doing their own music thing and it wasn't labeled by genre. I could leave the personal life and be a part of what was making me feel good and that was the music. No matter what was going on in my life, music always had the power to make me feel good. Not only that, but I had always stayed close to a minister because I know God has always had my back.

It was such a happy time because the music was good, the people were good, and life was good. I was ready to fully accept and embrace the title of the "Daughter of the Blues."

Chapter 8 - Big In Japan

I knew music and singing was the direction I wanted to go in, but I needed to develop my act. Just like with dancing, I had to come up with a performance that the crowd would enjoy. I had learned from Daddy that it's all about showmanship and professionalism. Moving into the singing world, I realized that there would be a lot of talk about comparing me to my father. From the jump, I made up my mind that this would be my show and I would do it my way. When I told Daddy what I was doing, he assured me that he was behind me and he was proud that one of his kids was also singing.

"I'm doing this my way, Daddy," I told him.

"Pretty girl, I would not expect anything different. I want you to make it on your own and always remember that it's a business. Show *business*."

"Yes, Daddy, I'll remember."

"It's tough and it's a man's world, baby girl. You have to be smart. There's a lot of con men out here."

I knew he was right. I'd been around long enough to realize that things could get real shaky if you deal with the wrong people. Hell, even if you deal with the right folks, money can get messed up and things can go sideways. He always stressed that the important thing is your reputation. I knew that with my name in people's mouths from dancing and being around town for a while that I had an advantage. I had been out of the spotlight for a minute and didn't want to wait too long before I got back in the game.

My old dancing friend, Malik, had become a good confidant when we met up in church, and the conversation always got back to music. I told him, "I'm working on getting my singing together. I've been practicing and I want it to be hot. First, I will need a good band."

I invited him to come to my show at the House of Blues. He walked in with a guitar. I knew he played keyboard, but I didn't know about the guitar. After the show, we started talking about the future.

"I have a song that I've written. A lot of them actually," he said.

"Oh, I didn't know you were writing. I'd love to hear it. Where are you staying?"

"If you like the song, I'll sell it to you. I can meet you back here later."

We met back up in Chicago, and I introduced Malik to a man named Pistol Pete, who was an amazing guitar player. He had worked with some of the best, so I figured if I was going to get my music going, I needed to go to the top. Pete had a studio and charged $20 a session. We went in and recorded the song Malik had written and it turned out real nice. I could see right away that he had talent, so I took him out to dinner to talk about the future.

"I need a bass player," I told him. "You think you could pick it up?"

"That's not really my thing, Shirley. Things have been a little tough for me. I don't even have an instrument. I usually just borrow one."

"You will soon," I told him. "Where you want me to send it?"

"Let's just meet up in a few days and I can get it from you."

In the meantime, I was working on my voice. I practiced at home in front of Patrick and Venus, and they gave me feedback. I could sing a few original songs, but people would want to hear their favorites, too, except I didn't want to do the same old thing.

I started messing with the arrangements and figuring out how to take the song, pull out the parts that I really connected to, and make them my own.

"That sounds good," Patrick said after I tried it out in our living room.

I was able to find a couple of other musicians, but I hadn't heard back from Malik. He was a good entertainer, so I was determined to get him in the band. When I finally did get a hold of him, there was good news and bad. He told me he was getting better at playing the bass I had bought for him, but what he hadn't told me is that he was homeless and living on the streets, sometimes staying at a shelter. He had also split from his wife. I could see the pain in his eyes.

"I really need the work, Shirley, but I don't think I'm as good as I should be."

"We're gonna fix that," I told him. I've had lots of nice folks help me out along the way and I was not going to turn my back on my old friend. "You will be in the band and I'll help you get where you need to be on the bass."

In the meantime, I got Malik some real nice clothes and took him to a different jam each night. I told him to pay attention to the bass player and see if he could do it. Finally he agreed to give it a shot. We were both single at the time and just had such a good time hanging out. We talked about being the next Ike and Tina, a dynamic duo ready to take on the Chicago music scene.

With my band together, I even hired another bass player temporarily. I told Malik he should watch this guy, learn from him, and work on his technique. It was just the boost that he needed. I could tell some of the other musicians didn't take to Malik because they knew he wasn't up to par, but this was my band and things would need to go my way. People started sending out rumors that we were hooked up and that's why I favored him. Oh, no, that was not true. I was not about to jeopardize my music. He asked me to let him go if it ever affected the performance, and I told him I would do that, but it was never necessary. I knew he needed help, but more importantly I had seen his talent. He just needed a little help getting there.

Once word got out that I had a band and was now singing, there was a lot of talk around town. Folks were excited to see me back on stage, because it had been a minute since I'd stopped dancing. There were also some tongues wagging about me trying to ride on Daddy's success. I expected as much, because it's natural for folks to doubt talent, especially when there were so many entertainers coming up at that time. It was important to earn my spot, and that's what I set out to do. Another thing working against me was my dancing career. People wanted me to keep on dancing and didn't want me to give it up, but it was too late for that.

The Shirley King Band (SKB) rehearsed seriously and I told the boys that they needed to sing, too, and interact with me and the audience. My kind of entertainment would be much more inclusive, just like the old-school days when it wasn't just the singing but the entire performance. I stressed to the band that people would probably turn out because of my name and who I am, but the band needs to show they have skills.

I told them, "This is my show, but it's *our show*, too. I want you guys to be recognized as top-notch musicians. Believe me, the audience will notice."

They did, too. Being in such a musical city, the Chicago audiences were very hip to what was going on and they knew talent. I was going to make sure we were right up there with the best.

I cranked myself into full business mode and was all in it. One of our first big shows was at the famous Kingston Mines on Halsted in Chicago, and things blew up from there. We got a standing ovation and we were on our way. Audiences loved the show, bookings jumped, and money started coming in. I was able to move over to the north side and get my kids into a nice place just like they deserved. They were also part of the business. Patrick came along to the clubs, passed out flyers for the shows, and talked to everyone about his mama's new band. It was so much like when I had been at Daddy's shows, as a kid. It was a different kind of life and one where they saw a lot of things going on. Patrick seemed to handle it well and he was a real help. He had a real love for the music. I tried to bring Venus into it, as well, even with some performing, but it wasn't her thing, which I understood.

My confidence wasn't real strong at first, but after we started getting such good responses, I became satisfied about our direction. Patrick was so excited and always gave me good feedback on how the shows were going. He loved seeing our lives change right before his eyes. I took him with us to a big show we had in Canada and it was amazing. We were getting many requests to perform across the country and even beyond. It was just crazy how things took off. Everything was working in my favor. I had my dancing name to work with and I used those skills to entertain while I sang.

Daddy's career had skyrocketed, too. He had received a medal from President George Bush and later was honored at the Kennedy Center by President Clinton. In the mid-1990s, he put out his own book, the story of his life, called *Blues All Around Me* co-written by David Ritz, who traveled and worked with him for about a year. I wasn't mentioned in that book because he didn't talk about any of his kids, but that was fine with me. There was no mistaking that every time he was in the news or on TV, it was a little boost for me and my band. He loved that because he always told me that I needed to make it on my own name, but if being associated with him helped, he was happy for that.

His life story coming out also helped his family to understand him better. Patrick said that he had never realized how much his grandfather had done and how hard he had worked. I took him and Venus to some of Daddy's shows, and, of course, we hung out with him backstage. He took Patrick on a tour of his bus and Patrick just loved it.

By the time Patrick was seventeen, my daddy asked him, "Do you want to see where the bus goes?"

I was a little cautious about that, but Daddy assured me that it would be good for him. I checked in with him often, but ultimately let him go on the road where he started learning the business and how much work it really is. He learned that the B. B. King show was a well-oiled machine, by then with several managers becoming very involved in his business affairs. Daddy was very trusting of them to handle things for him.

Patrick was in charge of filling in wherever he was needed. He helped with set up and break down of the shows, he got things that Daddy needed, and he coordinated the craziness that always went on backstage. My dad loved to visit with people after the show and he stayed for hours, giving everyone a chance to say hello. Patrick was a little young still, and that was a lot for him to handle, but it was for sure a learning experience.

In the meantime, we were popular overseas and even recorded a CD called *Jump through the Keyhole* on a Japanese record label. That was a big deal, because, at that time, getting a professional CD together meant that I had reached another level of success. I had big shows in Japan, Iceland, and England. The crowds seemed to grow larger and larger with each show and they were so enthusiastic.

For me, the ultimate highlight of touring came when we played the Umbria Jazz Festival in Italy, because the B. B. King Band was on the same bill. We opened for them and it was an amazing feeling for me to have come full circle. I had gone from longing to spend more time with my father to getting my band in the same festival as his. I knew that I would never be in his league, but it was rewarding to know that I had been able to come this far. If nothing else ever happened for me professionally, I was comforted by the fact that I had been able to put together a band, play a world tour, and even have my band open for my dad's band.

That was not only a career highlight but a personal one, too, because I knew that all of my hard work had paid off. I had not only earned the respect of the industry and the fans, but also of my father, the most important of all. If he trusted me to open his show, that was a nod of confidence from him. He loved that I was following in his footsteps with my own style. That support meant the world to me.

Despite all of that success, I was still trying to find myself. You know, it was an odd thing to feel so accepted all over the world and still not be able to control my own life. I could handle a huge audience with no problem; that was easy. Finding love and happiness in my personal life was damn near impossible. Maybe I was intimidating as a woman in the Blues world. I'm not sure why, but my love life just stressed me out. Not only that, but keeping the band going and the whole business part of things was a lot of work. I was making sure we got bookings, collecting the money, getting my musicians paid, and still trying to be a mother, too. It was a lot.

The real happiness I had was seeing that Patrick was getting a lot out of working with Daddy. He told me he met so many famous people—James Brown, Willie Nelson, Mike Tyson, a couple of U.S. presidents—it was a good way for him to learn the business. When he first started out doing that, I was even a little jealous, because it always seemed like other people got to spend more time with my dad than I did, but I got past that. I loved seeing my son dressed up real nice—like Daddy insisted—and collecting his weekly paycheck. He saw a lot that went on behind the scenes and how all kinds of people were always pulling at Daddy, wanting something from him . . . usually money.

Venus was older by that time and with Patrick working, I felt that things were a little more stable in this very unstable business. B.B. taught him what it was like to have money and how to manage it.

Patrick said one of Daddy's popular sayings was, "If you're not happy, you need to figure out why and do something about it." It was good for him to have a male role model in his life and I was so happy that it was working out. I flew out to a few of the shows and met up with Patrick to see how things were going.

"Mom, I'm learning a lot, that's for sure," he told me one night. "He's always trying to teach me things."

"That's wonderful, son," I told him.

"He always talks about you. Calls you his 'Shirley Ann.' If I say that my mom is driving me crazy, he says, 'Watch what you say, that's my daughter.'"

That made me smile. "And that's my daddy."

Daddy was always trying to help me after I got into the singing business. He mentored me, and any time I met him after one of his shows, he asked how things were going. "Don't let the little things get in your way. Pay attention to your business, and always come to me with questions."

Our relationship had evolved to another level. He was treating me as another performer, not as his daughter, and he was concerned for my success. When we were in the same town together, he usually introduced me on stage and sometimes invited me to sit in on a song or two.

Just as I started growing closer to him, my career was pulling me further away. I had commitments to keep and shows to do. Some people didn't like when I stuck up for myself, but I had learned from the best that this was a tough business, and even tougher for a woman.

I hit the road and toured up and down the east coast. We went out West, and we then did many shows in Canada. We always received such warm welcomes no matter what type of venue it was. I enjoyed the fact that I saw lots of White faces looking up at me from the audience along with the Black folks. It felt good to reach so many different kinds of people. I just wanted to make everyone happy, at least for an hour or two.

It was not always an easy gig, though. I still had to work for it and work hard. We played a Jazz gig once in a very fancy, upscale place, where the elite audience assured us they were "just here for the Jazz." During a break, Malik told me there was a lady rolling her eyes during my show, indicating that somehow it was beneath her. Whenever I heard something like that or got that kind of vibe from the audience, it just made me work harder, which is what I did. By the end of that show, they were all dancing, some on the chairs and tables, in their nice clothes.

"Your act is infectious," Malik said. "You always win them over."

Somehow, we got booked into a hard Rock club in Albany. I'm not sure how that happened, because it's a lot of work to keep those schedules booked at the right places while allowing for travel time. I started changing up the songs a little, giving them more of an edge. I told the band that if they were tight, we could get through anything. By the end of the night, the audience was singing along with me. That energy felt amazing and very satisfying.

While touring, Malik and I were really hitting it off. I always had a weakness for bass players and it was happening again. We were good together—real good—maybe too good. It seemed like whenever things got good personally and professionally, something just went left.

I was determined to keep the music going. I hustled for every show. We played at the Chicago Blues Fest and opened for Bonnie Raitt. I introduced Malik to Shirley Dixon, an amazing singer and daughter of Blues legend Willie Dixon. Shirley Dixon was on the phone with someone at the time. We heard the British accent through the mouthpiece. "It's Mick Jagger," she said. "He can wait."

As we toured around, we met and worked with all kinds of people—Robert Cray, Marcia Ball, and my daddy—Mr. B. B. King—it was just amazing. We went to Blues festivals and outdoor shows because there would be so many artists there, and magic music moments just happened on the spot. There were a couple of times when we hadn't gotten on the bill for some reason. I took

the guys, found a spot on the lawn, and start playing. I sang a capella, when I had to, and I attracted a crowd. I was always hustling.

Malik had come a long way as far as his playing skills and being
an entertainer. He was so nervous at first, and I knew it. I told him,
"If you mess up, do it big, make it part of the act, and play it up.
The audience will think it is part of the song. Once it's over, just
don't do it again."

Soon, Malik's confidence grew and he went from being appre-
hensive to gaining respect and helping manage the band. I took
him to some of Daddy's shows and introduced him as my boyfriend. Daddy was real nice to him, but he did not like those long
dreadlocks. Dad was from the old school, where you kept your
hair tight and your clothes sharp. This more casual style was not
his thing.

He always told Malik, "Take care of my daughter."

"Yes, sir."

Malik was amazed at how Daddy always remember people's
names when they came up to greet him. He knew that was part
of the job and he was real good at it. I usually went into little girl
mode around Daddy, because I always felt like his little girl, no
matter how old I got.

If he knew I was in the audience, no matter where I was, I came
running when I'd heard him yelling into the microphone, "Shirley!
Where's my Shirley? Come on up here!"

Usually when we went backstage, even though there were lots
of people trying to get to him, Daddy and I kept our ritual of going
off by ourselves to talk. I won't share all the things we discussed
because some were truly private, but he was always happy to give
me advice and he was just so proud that I was making my own
way. That thrilled him.

I was always meeting new people, and when I clicked with someone, I tried to keep them in my life, because it was hard to find
true friends in this tough business. When I met a man named Phil
Stark, I knew I had not just met a smart business man but a good
person, and that went for his wife Lora, as well. We hit it off immediately, and Phil helped with booking shows to keep me working.

One night, I was performing at a premier Detroit, Michigan club called Memphis Smoke. It was a real hot night and the air conditioning had gone out. Phil was nice enough to leave in the middle of the performance to go to Wal-Mart and buy a tall fan to put on stage. Those lights were about to burn me up. It was a hot, steamy show, but of course I still played it up and did my thing.

There was a man in the audience, who I started calling "Daddy." I told him to "come to mama" and the crowd just loved it. At the end of the show, this man was good and drunk and I guess he took things seriously. Just as we were breaking down the equipment, he came up and tried to hit on me.

"Oh, baby, that was just part of the show, and the show is over!" I said.

Well, he didn't want to hear none of that and he just kept it up.

"You see that man up there?" I asked, as I pointed to Malik, "Well, he's my husband." Then, I pointed at the drummer, guitar player, and the horn player. "See those other men there? Well, they my husbands, too!"

That was all it took to send him on his way.

In Ottawa, Canada, I had just finished a performance and was autographing some publicity photos for the fans. After I'd signed one of them, a man held his autographed picture in his hand like he was protecting it.

I told him, "Now don't go throwing any darts at that."

He responded real fast, "Oh, no!"

I looked him up and down and said, "And don't do nothin' else to that either!"

Everybody broke out laughing and he said, "You're bad, Shirley. You're bad."

I have dealt with a lot of media during my career with interviews, promotions, that kind of thing. I met a woman named Susan Blakes, who was covering a story about local Blues musicians. We talked and struck up a real friendship.

She told me about how she had met my father many times. "I saw him at a show in Milwaukee at the Potawatomi Casino and then in Rockford, Illinois. After one of those shows, during his meet and greet, I got to look at his bus. I was standing there by his grandson when B. B. picked up a camera to take a picture. I stepped out of the way and he lowered the camera. 'Get back in there,' he told me," she said with a smile.

Susan had a degree in psychology. She watched me perform, and I could tell she was assessing everything. She was very good at giving me advice and helping me stay strong in this difficult world of Blues music. It was often an uphill battle, and I've never really got the respect that a lot of the men got.

Because of Daddy's fame, I had so many people approaching me that I started getting real paranoid. I was careful about taking a drink from someone or being alone because there was talk about children of famous people getting held for ransom. Some people wanted to get close to me so they could get near my father. It started to mess with my head a little bit, because I had to meet people as part of my work, but it was scary.

When I got worried that Daddy was disappointed, Susan reassured me. "Your dad loves you. He kept you with his family growing up. That means something."

I was reluctant to go to his Milwaukee show, but with her support, we both went, and she was right. He was very excited to see me. He took my hand and we walked through the lobby of the hotel, and it felt like I was a child again being comforted by the most important man in the world—my father.

There were many fellow musicians who did support me along the way. It was important in that world, and especially in the Chicago Blues scene, for people to have my back. Ron Wright was one of those guys. I met him back in the 1990s, and we supported each other's music. I went to his shows, and he came to mine. We even invited each other up on stage if we could. It was about sharing the experience and the talent. He called me "the healer" because of the way I danced and talked with people, trying to make them feel good. He had met my father a few times, and he told me he could see that I had the same kind of spirit.

In 2000, Malik and I went with Phil and his wife to the Red, White, and Blues Festival in Marietta, Ohio. Phil was driving his Chevy SUV and he had booked three gigs for us. The first was at Bogarts in Parkersburg, West Virginia.

Then, I headlined at the festival in Marietta. Finally, we went to O'Hooley's in Athens, Ohio. Phil liked to get those bookings for me and he really did a good job this time. The trip through Ohio went smooth and we had all kinds of laughs along the way. We arrived in Parkersburg and had just enough time to check in to our hotel rooms, grab something to eat, and then arrive for a quick sound check before the show. I wasted no time in hopping on stage with Malik and starting the show. The crowd was kind of rough, but soon they were chanting "Shirley King, Shirley King!" I was always glad when we were able to win over a crowd. One down and two to go.

The next day, we got to Marietta, Ohio and stayed at a hotel on the riverfront. Everything was first-class all the way and the place was beautiful. There was a festive environment and that just carried on to the audience. The main stage was to the side of the hotel right there on Front Street. We went to the front desk to check in. Phil and Lora went to their room, and Malik and I to ours. When we got there, it was such a nice Victorian-style décor and there was a large, fragrant bouquet of flowers in a colorful vase sitting on the table with a "Thank You" note from the City of Marietta. That was so sweet.

Phil and Lora came to the room with news. Phil had a note requesting that I make an appearance at what they called a "garden party" the next day.

I was careful not to get into any strange situations, so I was a little leery. "What is a garden party anyway?"

Phil went to the front desk to do some investigating. He said that the clerk told him the guy hosting the party pretty much owned the town. He was said to be a little eccentric, but harmless. I told him to go ahead and let them know we would go, especially since they said they would send a limo to pick us up.

We did the show that day at the festival and everything went real well. The audience was lively and eager to party, so I was very happy with that. We even had two encores and calls for more, but I had to stop before we ate up the next performer's time. Can't do that!

The next day, Lora and I were in the spa wrapped from head to toe in spinach, an herbal wrap that we were trying.

Phil came running in all frantic, the way he got sometimes. He looked at us like we were crazy, and said, "Here comes Popeye!"

We got the message and went off to get ready, but I started having second thoughts. "I think we ought to cancel this and just be on our way." I told them how Daddy had always told me to pay attention to my surroundings. He was so protective and didn't want me around any craziness.

Phil finally just wore me down; he just didn't give up. I told him there were two conditions: one, we would follow them in Phil's SUV, and two, there would be no open drinks for me at the event. I know it stressed Phil out, but I was just not sure about this.

A man met us in the lobby and said he was the brother of the guy we were meeting and they had changed out the limo for a full-size van. Phil told the man our plans, and we were off. Just one hitch—Phil's car started acting up and stalled out. The van turned around and came back to find out what we were doing on the side of the road. I reminded Phil that we had the other performance at 9:00 that night in Athens. I was stressing out because I did not miss shows. That was just me. That was also one of Daddy's rules of being a professional. So, the SUV got towed away and we had to climb into that van.

I wasn't happy, but I was doing my best to keep my word and show up at this garden party thing. The man asked what we thought of the note that Phil had been given about this trip.

Lora spoke up. "It sounded like a ransom note!"

That got me worried. "Oh, no," I said.

Lora nudged me and patted her purse. "That's all right, we have protection."

The driver said, "Oh, are you packing?"

Lora said, "We're protected."

We arrived at a place that looked like nothing I had seen before. It was some sort of castle with big wooden doors in the front. As we entered, I was very cautious because that place was different. I saw a big bookshelf against the wall, and the guide showed us that if you push a button the wall turns around and changes into a full bar! That place was like some kind of funhouse. Then, we followed him down a tunnel into a wine cellar that ended up at a waterfall! It was like a fairy tale or something. I wasn't sure what to think.

Finally, they took us out to this garden they had been talking about. I was careful to only drink from unopened bottles, remembering Daddy's advice. Phil went off to check on his car, so Lora and I mingled with the interesting crowd. I was starting to get a little antsy about the next show. Lora tried her best to calm me down, but I was stressed out. I didn't like unpredictable situations like this. Too risky for me.

Phil came back with the bad news. "My SUV won't be ready until tomorrow."

I couldn't take it. "Oh no! What we gonna do now?"

Our hosts overheard and said we could take the large van if we needed it. We hopped right in and Phil jumped behind the wheel. They even gave us a cell phone. Man, these people were so nice, but that trip was just jinxed. First the cell phone started ringing, and since it was real new, we didn't know how to work the damn thing. We were all cussing at that little chirping phone. Finally it stopped.

Phil was able to re-dial the number. They told him that they had called and he actually had answered the last time. They heard every word of us cussing and fussing. I was covering my eyes, I was so embarrassed. Then, we stopped to get gas and didn't have the dang key for the gas tank. Phil went off to get some pliers and in the meantime, Miss Lora jumped out and wacked that cap real good and got it off! I don't know how we did it, but we finally got to the hotel and even took a little nap. I needed to relax after that crazy ride.

When it was time for the show, I got ready and headed downstairs. Come to find out, Phil had locked the keys in the van! Have mercy!

He called a cab, and we were getting in when we realized Malik's bass was locked in the van. I was going to have to sing a capella, and that wasn't what the club was expecting. Lora and I took that cab to the show and we got there just in time. I took that stage and started working the crowd, just riffing and goofing on them. After a little while, Phil and Malik came rolling in with the bass, the band started up, and we rocked that show!

After we wrapped everything up, a tow truck had gotten the key for us, and we were barreling down the road in that van, heading back to Marietta. Next thing I know, there were flashing blue lights behind us. Phil had gotten us pulled over by the cops.

He had a hell of a time trying to explain whose van that was, and just as he started trying to tell the long story, the cop just said he didn't feel like dealing with us since we had out of state license plates. I sure wasn't going to question that. Let's get home! Eventually, we picked up the SUV and the four of us headed home with many stories to tell.

My next gig was interesting in a different way. In Champaign, Illinois, we did a show for a school. I was interested in supporting the Arts in education, so this was a way to test the waters. The setup was different, and I lost my balance and fell off the stage! I was splayed out on the floor like a ragdoll and my ankle twisted almost clean off. The bone popped out and they had to pop it back in place and apply ice. I was in real pain, but I was also pissed because I couldn't finish the show.

We still kept our next gig in Washington, D.C. at Madam's Organ Blues Bar. I just had to perform in a wheelchair. The club owner told me it was amazing to watch the audience dancing and cheering along with a woman up on stage in a wheelchair. In Louisville, Kentucky, the mayor came up on stage to recognize me, and I tried to get him to sing. I liked playing around and having some fun, especially with the big shots, because the fans love that. I did finally get him to sing, and then he presented me with a key to the city. It was a big honor. I knew my dad's name got me in the door, but it was my performance that would get me asked back, and I tried my best every time.

I was laid up for a little while waiting for my ankle to heal. I had learned long ago when I was dancing that my body is important in my business. Pushing myself didn't do me any good. Unfortunately, since I was out of commission, so was the band. There was no Shirley King Band without Shirley, so the guys had to cool it for a while. Malik started to drift away for some reason. My dreams of our musical partnership began to evaporate, and Daddy was just fine with that. He never took to those baggy clothes and dreads.

Chapter 9 - Sick in Vegas

Like everywhere else, the Chicago music scene changed with the times and the fickle demands of the public. What folks liked at this point wasn't the same as a few years down the line. That's just how it went. While I was laid up after twisting my ankle, I took notice of how the scene was changing. I had paid my dues and earned my spot, but the Blues clubs were not as popular as before. There were more R&B and Soul establishments, especially with female performers. The Blues game was made up mostly of men, and they have been around for many years. Not only that, they were often descendants of Blues singers or musicians, so it was usually passed down the line, sort of like with me and my dad.

With the popularity of the R&B sound, things were getting a little tough. Through the 1990s and the 2000s, there was an explosion of new singers, such as Aaliyah, Mary J. Blige, Toni Braxton, India Arie, Erykah Badu, Kelly Price, and on and on. All of that new talent really changed the way audiences see performances. Just like back when I saw Etta James and it gave me an idea of how a stage show should look, the same was happening around 2003. While I did perform many Blues tunes, I also liked to do some music on the R&B tip, even working in some Al Green tunes at times to remind me of that history we shared.

I had to be careful changing my act too much, because my audience might not follow along. I knew so many musicians, who stayed the same and it worked for them. The legends, like Daddy, went a few different ways. They stayed in their lane and kept things going, making a decent living, or they tried to widen their audience. Daddy did that by hooking up with popular artists, such as U2 and Eric Clapton. He lent them some Blues cred, and they exposed him to a different audience. Some musicians created their own home base and that way they had their little piece of the music world that they controlled, because they made their mark.

I was trying different things to keep my show interesting, but I had to be careful. My daddy never had a problem letting me know he deserved respect. Once, I was booked at a place called Famous Dave's. It was the first one built and they wanted live music. The owners booked me because they knew Daddy was playing a show in town and they wanted to use me and my name to get an audience. They probably hoped Daddy would show up to see me and help bring even more of a crowd. The place did fill up for my show, and I started performing like usual. Everyone was getting into it and things was going real smooth, then all of a sudden I was singing to empty chairs! Every person in there had left. I thought, *Now, what the hell done happened?* Come to find out, Daddy had come in the back door, passed right through the restaurant, and kept on going. Well, everyone jumped up and followed along behind him. I just thought, *Okay, Daddy, I got the message.* He wanted to make his point in a gentle way. After that, I stopped trying to book shows near his or piggyback on any of his gigs. I could be stubborn at times, but not where Daddy was concerned.

Being around my father, I did notice that things were changing around him, especially his management. They were becoming much more controlling as he got older, and he became more reliant on them. It was more difficult to see him, and family events became less and less frequent. Not only that, I could see that his memory was a little shaky. In 2005, it was becoming obvious that his age was catching up to him. I didn't have a good feeling about his situation. Despite everything, Daddy was still playing and even did a show in his hometown of Indianola on his eightieth birthday. He sat in on a gig with my old friend, Billy Branch.

Professionally, things were going a little sideways for me. First, I met up with a nice woman, who helped guide me and pull together a CD that was for sale in all the big stores. Next thing I knew, she was getting too friendly with me. After I shut that down, she pulled all of the music off the shelves, and with it my hopes for a career boost. It was always very tough to find people I could completely trust in this business. There was lots of good folk and a lot of swindlers. I started to realize that I needed to work a little harder to get back on track. That foot injury had sidelined me for a while, and once I was out, people were real quick to forget me.

I was learning that the old saying was true: struggle is the cousin to hustle. I needed to get my hustle back.

I was able to book more overseas shows. There was an annual festival in Germany that brought thousands of people, and I was the headliner there. I also played Portugal and Brazil. Those places love their Blues music and outdoor festivals. It was a lot of fun to see such lively, appreciative audiences.

Meantime, Daddy had made his home in Las Vegas, so I'd try to spend as much time with him as I could. In the past, he always sent me a ticket or some travel money. As my dad, he wanted to provide and help me, which was wonderful. He made sure there was a place for me to stay and provided a car. Everything was taken care of in advance. He was always a class act.

Things began to change around 2009. There was less communication and he was depending even more on those around him. He was all but cut off from his family. He told me that he couldn't send me a ticket because he was running out of money. He started crying because he thought he was letting his family down. It wasn't the actual ticket that was the issue, it was that he couldn't pay my way to his show. It was a matter of pride for him because he was under the impression that he didn't have any money left. Any time I did get to see him, especially after a show, he wanted to stay up all night in the hotel room just talking. He rarely slept, mostly just little catnaps during the day. I don't know how he did it, but he did.

Often, I was able to see him on my birthday and that made it all the more special. On my sixty-third birthday, I was with him, because, for once, he was not working that night. I was able to hang out with him and talk to him, and it reinforced to me how important it was to have a father in my life at any age.

I told him I didn't think my new relationship, the one he had blessed, was for me.

My father said, "Baby, it's up to you, but you know it's hard to have a good relationship in this business. Not everyone understands what you have to do. I haven't found that yet myself. I deal with women and they know what I'm doing. After a while, they want me to stop doing what I'm doing, so that's why your dad is not in a relationship. Music and relationships does not go together."

I said, "Daddy, I'm with someone who does what I do."

He said, "It doesn't matter. In this business, you are obligated to it and nothing else."

My dad was right. I'm so glad I had those private, precious moments with him when he could just be my father. In 2010, I celebrated my next birthday with a friend, who had me come and perform in Massachusetts near where Daddy was playing a gig. I was able to go be with him after my show. It wasn't the best party, because people by then had stared to divide and conquer. I spent a whole day trying to get to see him. It wasn't easy, but by the time I got to my dad, he put me up in a nice room, gave me money to buy myself a gift, and that night announced that he wanted the audience to sing to me. They sang "Happy Birthday, Shirley" and gave me an ovation. Then, my father sang to me his song, "Guess Who?" which tells how much someone loves you. Oh my God, how special that was. It was beautiful. That was another great birthday celebration with my dad. Not only did he say he loved me, but he showed me. He always did. My daddy was a promise keeper.

One of the best things for my career was that I booked a steady gig at a private club called The Joynt, owned by a guy named Stan. He was connected to lots of people, even having worked with Frank Sinatra at one point. When I did shows at The Joynt, I met a lot of interesting, high-profile people. It was very exciting and there was always someone coming up to me after one of my shows.

Any time I got a chance to travel on tour with Daddy, I took it. It was so fun to watch him work and see how he had created such a fine-tuned machine. He knew exactly what worked for him and what didn't. I couldn't travel in Big Red with the boys, but that was fine with me as long as I got to be around Dad. I got to spend about six months with him. We were at a show in southern Illinois when I started getting pains. I had already gone through menopause, but I started bleeding and knew something wasn't right.

I never had any problem talking with my father. He'd seen me through a lot and had always been supportive, so I went and told him that something didn't feel right. He sent me right off to a local doctor to get checked out. They couldn't find anything, so when I got home, Daddy said to make sure to keep an eye on things. I went to the Rush University Medical Center and, once again, the doctor didn't detect any issues, but he ran some tests. The day I got called to come back for the results, I felt like something was strange. I'm not really superstitious, but it was April 1, 2009, April Fool's Day, and as I was going into the clinic a black cat ran in front of me.

The doctor said I had Stage 3 uterine cancer and it had spread to my lymph nodes. I felt like I'd been hit by a bomb. I folded for about eight days. I couldn't talk, couldn't cry, couldn't sleep; nothing. It was like I was stuck somewhere in the middle of reality. Nothing made sense anymore. As an entertainer, I'd never had any real paycheck and, of course, no insurance, so I wasn't sure what that meant for my future. I wanted to take care of myself, but what could I do? The doctor kept trying to get in touch with me, and finally he did. He told me I needed to go to the hospital immediately.

When I did go, I met with another doctor, the one in charge of the cancer unit. I let him know why I was so worried. "I have no insurance. I am a performer. Don't even get me started wasting your time with me. I know I'm going to die."

He didn't like that. He snapped. He told me there are ways to make sure I was covered and that his priority was to get me better, not to make money. He was not putting up with my mess, that's for sure. He got me into a program called Charity Care that helped me afford the surgery so I wouldn't have to go through the system to try and get coverage. I was fortunate that this was one of the top hospitals in the country when it came to cancer care.

On May 12, 2009, the doctor got me into surgery for a hysterectomy. Then, I started a year of chemo treatments through 2010. That was a rough time. They had to give me extra-strong doses because the cancer had spread to my lymph nodes. It took a good two years of treatments, off and on, before they finally told me it was in remission. I developed a good friendship with the doctor who had lost his patience with me, and he has been helpful any time I've had questions. The final step was that I needed to have the port in my chest removed. That's the part where they administered the chemo. They need to make certain it hadn't returned. So, until they were satisfied that I was through with the cancer, I kept a souvenir of the most horrible time of my life.

This industry made me tough on the outside, that's for sure, but I guess it also toughened up my insides, because I was able to get through the cancer thing and come out on the other side.

I thought my next move might be acting in a movie. I was always trying to think of the business aspect of entertaining and trying to reach more people. That was my next vision, my next dream, my next hope: to play a nightclub singer in a movie. I had come very close around 2000, but that opportunity fizzled out. While I was playing at The Joynt, Blues dancing was becoming real popular. It's a type of dance that went way back to those days back in the juke joints. It has changed over the years, and was then similar to the "dirty dancing" style, but to Blues music.

An independent movie called *Chi-Town Pulse* (2010) was filmed at the club, and they asked me to play the singer, which I thought was a lot of fun. Just by playing that part it felt like I was accomplishing things I had wanted to do. The goal I had set to be in another movie came true, despite dealing with my health issues. When I went to the premier, I was quite impressed, because they did the red carpet and TV interviews. It was big deal in Chicago. I performed at the party after the film was shown. I was in my fancy stage outfit, complete with a feather headdress. It was amazing to see so many younger people still have love for the Blues.

At first, I wasn't sure what was going on with me. Things were picking up with my career once again, and I was getting calls to perform at shows like I used to, especially outdoor festivals. I wanted to sing and perform, but it just became harder and harder to get that motivation. It was like I was pulled in two directions. I wanted to do the shows in my mind, but I just felt physically weak. I had recovered from the cancer, but with the stress of seeing my father's health get worse and being almost cut off from him, my world just felt dark. That's the only way to describe what I later found out was depression. I'd been upset and angry, but I don't think I'd ever been clinically depressed, at least not like this. It was just a horrible feeling of nothingness. My heart was empty.

This was not good for me or my career. I needed to just get out and make myself available. I needed to stop focusing on things I could not control and start letting positive people into my life. I've always been one who could shut myself away and it would be like I'd fallen off the planet. I was good at going ghost. One day I was here and the next day it was "Where's Shirley? Has anyone heard from her?" With Daddy being sick and the rest of my family doing their own thing, it felt like it was me against the world. Then, I realized it was time to adjust my attitude and my life. So, I said yes to the outdoor festivals and to the invites to sit in on shows. Anything to get my behind out of the house and on the stage.

People came up to me all of the time after a show to tell me how they enjoyed it and sometimes to talk about Daddy. Either way, I loved connecting with people. That's really what fed my soul and gave me the strength to keep going.

After one outdoor show, a nice woman came up to me. "I just loved the concert. You were great. I really enjoy your music."

"Thank you so much. What's your name?"

"I'm Susan. Susan Jablonski."

"It's wonderful to meet you."

We talked for a while and really struck up a friendship. We talked about everything from relationships, to the music business. Just everything.

"This might be kind of strange, but I'm having a barbecue coming up and I'm wondering if you'd like to come."

"Oh, to perform?"

"No, just as a friend."

We just fed off each other's positive energy. She even started coming with me to see Daddy whenever he had a show nearby. The first time we went was wonderful. Daddy took Susan on a tour of his bus and we went backstage. Daddy looked healthy and in great spirits.

Then, we went to a show in Aurora, Arkansas, and I also had my granddaughter, Jasmine, with us. I wanted her to see her great-grandfather on stage. That was one of the first times where I was not even allowed to see my father. He always left us some nice tickets, but at this show they only gave us two tickets and they were way in the back. It was frustrating and embarrassing for me. Susan tried to console me, but it wasn't just this concert that concerned me. I knew things were getting much worse, but I still had to focus on making that green paper.

Every summer, the city of Chicago held the Chicago Blues Festival—it had a thirty-year tradition. For the past few years, I got a call from a lady named Joan Gand. She and her husband were musicians with a band of their own, The Gand Band. They had been playing together since the early 1970s and they were true lovers of all kinds of music, especially the Blues. Joan played keyboard and Gary played on the six strings. They really worked to preserve that old school sound and the classic way of performing.

Joan first called me back around 2010, just a year after the amazing "Queen of the Blues" Koko Taylor passed, away and told me about her idea. "The Chicago Blues Festival hasn't planned an event to honor Koko. Also, for some reason, there are no women on this year's roster of performers. It's probably an oversight, but a lot of people have mentioned it."

"So what are you thinking, Joan?"

"If no one else is going to do it, I will. I've talked to Reggie's and they have a large space where they agreed to host a women's Blues festival that will start after the Chicago festival. It will have ten divas and cost $10."

Now, I loved the idea, and I can tell you it was tough out there for a woman in music, but on that date I was going to see Daddy's show in Memphis. He headlined a festival there every year, so even though I wanted to do it, I had to support Daddy. Bless her heart, Joan called me every year asking if I could join the ladies on stage.

While I was still work at The Joynt, another movie was filmed there, and my music was featured in it. It was called *Chicago Mirage* (2011) and was produced and created by a man from Hollywood, who was had also acted in movies, such as *Iron Man* (2008). He was a friend of the club owner. He heard about me, and they came and saw the show, and decided to have me sing on the soundtrack, another honor, because to be recognized vocally, that was something I hadn't thought about, but I was happy I did it. It did well in many film festivals and there's my voice on the soundtrack. My career often felt like a see-saw; it would go up and down, and so did my respect in this business.

Buddy Guy was a legend in the industry and a Chicagoan through and through. He had his own club in the city. He always worked hard to stay close to my dad, but for some reason he never paid me much attention. That happened sometimes in the music game. I don't know if it's the female thing or the famous father, but sometimes I got love when Daddy was around, but as soon as he left, I was like a pretty ghost. Some folks just pretended I didn't exist. That was hard to understand.

One night, Daddy took me to Buddy's club. It was 2012 and Daddy was playing a big show in the city. When I knew he was going to be in town, I made sure I didn't take jobs that night. I preferred to see him and spend time with him, so I kept my schedule open when he was around. That night, he was playing at the House of Blues, and George Benson came by to sit in with him. Buddy Guy asked my dad to come see him at his club after the show.

I was standing beside Big Red when Daddy came through, grabbed my hand, and took me on the bus with him. We drove to Buddy's club and everyone knew when B. B. King arrived, because even though he had taken his name off Big Red, there was no mistaking it. I got off the tour bus holding Daddy's hand. Buddy walked up to us, hugged my dad, and pushed me to the side. I was shocked. I wanted to say something to Dad, but I realized I didn't need to. My father was very smart about how people act. He paid close attention and then didn't say anything. He dealt with it his way.

When we were in the club, a woman came out from the kitchen.

Buddy said, "B. B., I'd like you to meet my daughter."

Daddy said, "Buddy, do you know this is my daughter?"

I was smiling because I knew what he was doing. He was making a point.

"Yeah, I do," Buddy said, and then he started talking about something else, but Daddy wasn't satisfied.

"Honey, do you know Buddy Guy?"

I said, "Yes, sir."

"Kiss him."

What? I didn't want to do that, but you know what? I wasn't going to disobey my dad. I did what he told me to do.

When I sat in on sets at Buddy's club when Daddy wasn't around, and I started singing, Buddy got up to leave. I'm not sure why, because I had never been disrespectful, but word got back to my daddy. He was not about to let someone disrespect me in his presence. Daddy was amazing like that and not just with me. It didn't matter that he had a tough struggle growing up and making a living. When he became a big superstar, he was still always looking out for others. He expected people to act decent and didn't put up with foolishness. It was obvious that musicians and others in the industry were envious of me singing on stage with my father. It wasn't because they thought I didn't have talent, but they wanted to take my place. He knew I would have it tough, so he did his best to open doors and help me without being so direct about it. Like he always said, I could use the B. B. King name up to a point, and then it was on me.

Later on at the club, everyone was all over my dad. People loved him. Buddy took my father over to a table filled with his family and friends. George Benson had ridden over on the bus with us and he was at the table, as well. I was left standing there by myself. Someone saw me all alone and asked if I would like to sit with them. They just happened to have a table in front of the stage. I saw my dad look over at me and I could tell he knew what I was dealing with. I've learned how to deal with the hurt. He always told me, "Just be strong." We were very spiritually connected and I knew he wasn't finished making his point that night.

After dinner, the three of them—Buddy, George, and Daddy—took the stage. Every musician in Chicago had tried to play there that night in hopes that Mr. King would sit in. So, the band started jamming and the three men did a few songs to the delight of the pleasantly surprised crowd. This was a real treat for them and a magical moment in music, as well.

When they had finished, Buddy got off stage first and George followed. Daddy was always a little slower, so he trailed behind.

Just then, once the other two were offstage, Daddy bent down and picked up the microphone. "Ladies and Gentlemen, I have my beautiful daughter here tonight. Most of you know she lives here in Chicago. She does the same thing her old dad does. I hope you don't mind if I call *my* daughter up here. Would that be all right with you all?" He always asked the audience for permission, and they just went crazy. They wanted to see us together. I was on the verge of tears. It's one of the highest points of my career because it meant everything to me, personally and professionally, coming from my father like that.

We took the stage. He got a chair and sat down with a glass of champagne beside him. Someone brought one for me, too. He looked at me in that adoring, fatherly way and smiled, my eyes moist with tears. We started singing "The Thrill is Gone." The band sounded really good. I knew all of the guys from around town. My dad was like a teacher on stage with me. He started singing and I remembered what he had told me before: "When someone asks you to jam with them, mellow in. Don't get totally excited and go off."

That was an important lesson, because the first time I had sat in with him, I did just that. I got carried away and he checked me. The next time I did it much differently and this made the third time he and I had taken a stage together. That very day, my daddy was passing me the torch, because he knew things were going downhill health wise.

That one moment will be branded in my mind forever. When he passed me his champagne glass, I took a sip and passed it back to him. Then, he leaned in and I gave him a kiss. I was in Heaven. I was honored to be treated so nice by him. The audience was going crazy. After we started singing the song, he kept hinting for me to sing more of it. So, I took it and did one verse, then I handed the mic to a guy in the band who wanted to join in. I don't think Daddy had that in mind, because he gave me a look, but it was okay in the end. I wanted to share the experience like he was doing with me. Once we finished the song, he gave me a kiss and I closed the song out. He got up, grabbed my hand, and we took a bow together. It meant the world to me. It was such a life-affirming moment.

Daddy had been getting weaker and weaker. I didn't know the full extent of it because the folks around him had tightened things up. Family was given little, if any, access to him except for Patrick. My son was out in Las Vegas working with Daddy, so I did feel a little better that at least some family was around him. That's why I was so excited to see him come to Chicago. He was set to play on October 3, 2014 at the House of Blues. Everyone was thrilled because we would all get to see him. I was hoping it would help reduce my anxiety levels since between worrying about him, having troubles with my man, and performing my own shows I knew my health could be in jeopardy and I didn't need any more of that.

I pulled some of my friends together for the show. Susan came with me and we were able to get seats on the upper level right over the stage. It was a great spot to watch my father perform. He had just turned eighty-nine, and I was excited to see how he was doing. It had been in the news that he had trouble with a show a few months earlier in St. Louis. He was weak and apparently not playing like usual. It was horrible to hear that, so I had high hopes that he would show all of us that he was ready to run that stage.

That was not the case. I could see from the start that he looked distracted and weak. I was in the VIP box seat right above the stage, so I could see him waiting in the wings and it looked like he was trying to get off the stage. I had never seen him act like that. Finally, he was walked out and propped up in his chair. He put his hands on his knees and just stared out at the audience. He did not have that usual fire that he had when he took the stage. That was where he usually came to life, but not this time. I felt sick to my stomach as I watched him struggle through a few songs. Then before I knew it, he just fell over and it was mayhem. There was a frenzy on the stage as handlers rushed in to usher him behind the curtains.

I had to suppress the urge to jump right off that balcony and try to help him. It was the most paralyzing feeling to realize I could only watch from a distance. Susan and I went down to the lobby and tried to get backstage, but they wouldn't let us in. It was so frustrating and not only that, I was worried sick. They said it wasn't serious and asked if we would go get him some food. I said of course. When we returned and waited in the lobby to go see him, they came out, grabbed the food, and shut the door without even a thank you.

I yelled after them, "Why do you have my dad sitting on that stage in that condition?" I was tore up.

There's a community center not far from my house used mostly by baby boomers and mature seniors to socialize and also get health care. I was feeling down and not sure what to do, so I went in there to use the public computers. I was up on Facebook trying to find out anything I could about Daddy and his condition. I wasn't sure what I could do, but I had to figure out something.

"Hi, I'm Dick Larkin. Nice to meet you."

I was just in the middle of reading some stories about the horrible news about Daddy and his health when I turned around to see this professional-looking White man smiling at me.

"I'm just using the computer. It's for the public, right?"

"Yes, that's fine. I hear you are B. B. King's daughter."

"Yes, I am."

"Do you sing?"

I happened to have some of my promotional postcards with me because I'm always hustling, so I gave him one. I felt comfortable with him and began a nice conversation. I told him about Daddy and his health issues and how I was worried about how he was being treated. I also talked a little about my cancer scare. He was very easy to talk to. We ran into each other off and on whenever I visited the center. It felt good to have someone to confide in.

Despite being worried about Daddy's health and getting practically no information, I tried to stick with my plan and keep working to make sure I didn't fall back into getting down and depressed about everything. Work always helped me feel good.

Joan Gand caught up with me and asked if I'd be interested in playing a show in Palm Springs, California. She goes down there to escape the crazy Chicago winter and, of course, play music around town. She brought me in to play a show at the Purple

Room right in the middle of town. The beautiful palm trees and warm weather reminded me of my days growing up in Los Angeles. It was late November, and I played two sold-out shows. It was amazing and just what I needed. The Gand Band was great, the audience was very enthusiastic, and it was a lively vibe. It is usually a supper club, but that night I had them move the tables aside and turn that place into a disco.

Joan knew that Daddy was sick. Of course, she had heard about what happened at the House of Blues. Then, I got a call from one of my sisters. She was crying and saying that things were getting worse. Joan told me to go see him.

"Shirley, Las Vegas is not too far from Palm Springs. Why don't you go visit him while you are out here?"

"To be honest, I'm not even sure they would let me see him. Plus, I have no way to get out there."

"We can make that happen," Joan said with a smile.

She did just that. A lady at the club had offered to assist with transportation to Vegas. Joan stepped in to help work it out so I had a way to see my dad. Then, the plan was that since our shows had gone so well, I would come back in a few weeks and play again at The Purple Room again.

Once I got there, I faced roadblocks every time I tried to get to see him. I found myself stranded in Las Vegas. First, I stayed with my ex-sister in law. We had a good relationship. Things were hard for working people in that town. It wasn't all glitz and celebrities. There were many musicians playing on the streets because there weren't enough jobs. They were living day by day. I spent my time going between people's houses. Some were tight on money, but they let me stay for a little while as I tried to get to my father. I wasn't about to give up on him. There was one friend who would take me and his wife to parties where we could get free food. That was sometimes my only chance to have a decent meal since my money was low.

Finally, I got the chance to see Daddy. He seemed miserable. He couldn't sit up, he was unshaven, and his pajamas were dirty. He looked so frail and tired that it almost made me cry on the spot.

I was able to give him a quick kiss on the cheek, but then I was escorted out.

It took another week or so, but I managed to get another visit. This time, I told them I wanted time alone with my father. They waited downstairs, listening the whole time. When I got there, he seemed to be doing better, sitting up, and kind of talking as though he was okay. I didn't realize that he had Alzheimer's and it was as bad as it was at the time, so I just thought he was tired. He loved watching old movies, especially cartoons and Westerns. So, as the movie played, we sat silently, loving each other through the spirit. After the movie, I told him about how great the Palm Springs show was and said I wished he could come there and do a show with me.

He said, "Baby, your daddy is tired and I don't know if that's going to happen, but tell them B. B. said he loves them."

It was very sad. I got up and rubbed his head and couldn't believe the shape he was in. He never dressed down, and now he was in tattered pajamas. He eyes looked glazed over. He got up and walked over to the window, looked out, and then sat back on the bed.

I said, "Dad, I'm sorry we didn't get to do a lot of things together, but I hope you're proud of me. I have worked hard to make you happy."

He said, "Baby, I'm very proud of you. If there was such a thing as a father having success, you are my success."

I said, "I would like something from you. If I could have a few of your coats to keep, that would mean a lot to me."

He said, "Sure."

I thought, 'Oh my God, he's really sick!' Those coats were important to him. He really admired his look and took pride in his appearance. If he realized the way he looked at that moment, he would have been mortified. He always said, "Appearance means everything. You never know where the cameras are." He always thought it was the right thing to do, to always take care of his appearance when he was out anywhere. When he told me I could have the coats, I almost fainted. I knew then that if he was willing to part with that, it was real bad.

I went in the room where he had nothing but rows and rows of show clothes. It looked like 1,000 coats. I walked in and selected three of them, walked back down the hallway, and the first coat I had on he said, "Oh no baby, not that one."

It made me laugh for the first time that day. I thought, *B. B. King is coming alive!* By the time I went to get another coat, a lady came upstairs. I explained that Daddy said I could have the coat. My dad looked up at her and said, "I told her she could have the coats."

She looked at him and said, "I told her she couldn't have them."

I knew something was not right. This woman was talking to him like a child, not like he was B. B. King. I didn't want to make things bad for him, so I just said okay. I didn't want to argue. I'd just wait until later. In the past, my dad always had a briefcase filled with money that he would share, but that was gone. His stuff was under their control now. I waited for a call about those coats, but I never got it.

They wanted me to leave Las Vegas, but it was almost Christmas, so I was asking some of our family out there if they wanted to come have Christmas with dad. One of them agreed and gave me a ride over to see him once again. He was sitting up and seemed to be in a little bit better spirits. It was just good to spend a little more time with him.

"You know, William Morris fired me because of those gigs," Daddy said.

"They fired you? Why? I mean, Dad, you give it the best you could. You can't do it anymore like that."

He said, "I said fuck 'em, because I have to take care of myself."

He rarely let people know what was really going on with him, but when he said that, I said, "Dad, don't worry about nobody. Just worry about getting better." I was looking at him and seeing his bones poking through his skin.

It was a difficult trip, but I had to get back to Palm Springs to perform. Daddy would never want me to miss a commitment. That was never even an option. When I got back, Joan knew it was bad.

"Shirley, you're like a different person. Are you okay?"

"It was a lot to deal with, Joan." I filled her in and she listened very patiently.

"Let's go shopping," she said.

That Joan was a positive force, I can say that for sure. We both picked out some nice clothes. Along the way, we talked to people and told them to come to the show that evening. I kept that hustle alive, that's the truth.

Once again, when I took the stage, it was like my worries just drifted away. Of course, they weren't totally gone, but I was able to channel all of that into the performance. It was probably the best therapy I could have gotten. The positive response from the audience gave me the boost I needed. The town was filled with older folk and a large gay population, and both usually responded well to my act. One man even came up and we did a little duet. I just had an amazing time and the ability to stop worrying about Daddy for a few hours was priceless.

After I got back to Chicago, legal things with Daddy started going all kinds of sideways. My sisters became involved and tried to confront the woman managing Daddy's business. They even took her to court in April of 2014. They lost that case and then went back again as Daddy got sicker. One day, they managed to get Dad out of the house and take him to the hospital. His business folk really got upset with them, because they didn't want him to go to the hospital. My sisters told me they wanted to get him out of the house because they weren't sure what was going on. It was beginning to look fishy.

I went back to the community center and started reaching out on Facebook to see if anyone could help us. I didn't want to get into anything legal, but I did want to make sure my father was not being mistreated. I created a page called "B. B. King's stories" and tried to reach some of the famous people who were saying they couldn't get in touch or talk to my dad. I cried out on Facebook, "Somebody please help my dad." That's as much as I got involved with it because I didn't know who was telling the truth and who was stringing me along.

I saw my friend, Dick, at the center again and told him what had been happening. I asked if there was anything they could do to help us out. I felt so powerless.

"We can't get directly involved," he told me, "but we will make a referral to a social worker near him in Nevada and see if anything can be done."

I was so appreciative, and apparently someone did check on him, so it made me feel a little better that they did not find anything to report during that time. Dick also brought up something else.

"Shirley, I have an idea. Would you be interested in singing at one of our centers, maybe at a birthday party? Is that something you'd consider?"

I said I'd give it a try.

"But first, you need to get your health insurance together."

"Oh I tried that before," I told him. "Since I never had a steady job, I don't qualify for any type of health program."

"That's not true. I need you to fill out the forms and apply so you can stay healthy."

I gave him some pushback, but he wasn't having it, and soon I found myself with regular healthcare just like a normal civilian! Performers are not used to having benefits like that.

There was an Oak Street Health Center on 87th Street in Ashburn. Dick said we would schedule a show there, invite anyone who had a birthday that month, and see how it went. I could see he wanted to put me to the test and see if I could do it.

The day of the show, I drove up in full performance attire and I brought a bunch of photos and memorabilia about my dad. They had a little microphone set up and I did what I do. I sang, I talked, and I shared some stories about my life and my father. After the show, Dick came up to me.

"Shirley, that was amazing. I saw you transform into a totally different person. I also noticed that the crowd loved it. They really connected with you. We have something here."

We did another show. And another. And another. Soon we had a monthly schedule where I was traveling between the seven different centers to perform for that month's birthdays. Dick told me that one of the centers, the one over near Garfield Park, was kind of a tough neighborhood and the show might not go over real well there. When we got there, it was a line out the door of people waiting to get in. There wasn't enough room for all of them.

The work was not only satisfying to me as a performer, but it was therapeutic because it helped me escape the worry for just a little while. Seeing those people smile and laugh just made my day. At the beginning of the show, they were sort of still and tired-looking, but by the end, they were set free! It was like the sun came out on a cloudy day. Nothing made me happier than seeing that pure joy, the way they lost themselves in the music and forgot their aches and pains.

On May 15, 2015, at about 1:00 in the morning, I received a call that I'll never forget. It was a reporter from Los Angeles.

"Hello?"

"Shirley?"

"Yes?"

"Is it true that your father has passed away?"

CHAPTER 10 - THE THRILL LIVES ON

My son was out in Vegas, and he told me he found out that my father had died when a friend called him and said, "Sorry to hear about that."

Patrick said, "What?"

He said, "Your grandfather."

The day before, I had asked Patrick to check on him. He called over to the offices, and the secretary said Daddy was fine. The next day, he was pronounced dead. When Patrick confronted her, she said she was told what to say.

I went out to Vegas and we all went to the funeral, but it was just a jumbled mess. It felt rushed and disrespectful. There was no communication about where it was even being held. We had to find out on our own. Even then, it was just lackluster. There was no thought in it. It was like no one cared anymore. My dad's body was lying in that mortuary when he should have been at one of the nicest venues in town where his body could have been available for a public viewing. Instead, they had him tucked away where you couldn't hardly see him good. Then, they had to do the autopsy because people started talking about him being killed and everything. Instead of me being there during that, I wanted to celebrate his spirit. Instead of being around that negativity, I contacted one of the clubs and set up a tribute show for him. I did something creative instead of just feeling sad. Performing is something Daddy would always respect. I had already told them I wouldn't dare fight when my daddy's body was being moved around and hadn't been put to rest. It was a matter of respect.

I stayed out of any legal issues, and I told my sisters to do the same, but they wouldn't listen. In the original will, Daddy had it set up for all fifteen of his kids to get $10,000 annually. That wasn't a lot, but it was a nice gesture. After his death, there was suddenly a new will that said each child got a one-time payout of between $2,000 to $5,000. I'd never heard of that will, but his business managers claimed it was valid.

One of Daddy's faults was that he was great with advice to others, but sometimes didn't take it himself. He always warned me about those pimps and other untrustworthy people, but then he would go and put all of his trust in someone without question. That was not always the best thing to do. A dead man can't talk, can he? At this point, I had to get on with my life. I preferred to do what I had to do. I didn't want none of that fighting.

Patrick told me that once, at a show in North Carolina in 2014, he had seen Daddy fall in a bathroom. He was dazed, but he tried to hide it and prove he was okay. Then, over Christmas of that year, Patrick said that Daddy looked at him like he was trying to figure out who he was. Then he said to Patrick, "Look at those teeth." Patrick said by the time he found out Dad was gone, half of his things had already been sold. It just broke my heart. My son always went to his grandfather for advice and wisdom, and suddenly he was alone.

Here's a timeline of how things played out up to the end.

April 7, 2014 – I went on Facebook and thanked everyone for supporting B. B. King, because he was having trouble on stage and couldn't focus. It was all over the news. He would forget what he was doing. I had gone to see him to make sure he was all right, but I wasn't allowed access. They had taken full control over his life. It would have never happened in the good days.

October 3, 2014 – That was the date of his horrible fall at The House of Blues in Chicago. I witnessed him not wanting to go onstage because he didn't want to embarrass himself. After the fall, he was rushed onto his bus and taken back to Vegas. He wasn't even allowed to go to a local hospital. There was nothing I could do. It was a painful night.

October 7, 2014 - A Facebook posting supposedly from my father read: "I am back at home now, listening to music, watching movies, and enjoying being at home."

October 9, 2014 - B. B. King was featured in a national commercial for Toyota. It was notable because it was about a girl finding a Lucille guitar and returning it to my father. Apparently, there were some legal issues that arose from that.

Christmas Day 2014 – I stayed for a month in Vegas and was able to see him on three separate occasions. The last time I ever saw him alive was on that day.

May 1, 2015 – A Facebook posting supposedly attributed to my father read: "I'm in home hospice care at my residence in Las Vegas. Thanks to all for your well wishes and prayers."

May 14, 2015 – At 9:00 p.m. he got tired and let go. I wasn't called and told. I got the news through a reporter. That feeling will never go away. I wanted to hold his hand while he was leaving this Earth, but didn't get that chance. It got so messy in the end, and it didn't have to be like that.

I was able to say yes to Joan's Women's Blues Festival a couple of times and it was always amazing. At the first show I did with them, the organizers had never seen one of my performances, but they loved spontaneous shows where musical magic happened. I was the right performer for that because I just let loose—not too much was planned when I took the stage. Joan said she wanted to allow me to shine without any constraints. So, I turned on the shine and the audience seemed to really like it. I love playing with the other ladies on the bill and the female musicians, too. It was so different from the way things used to be way back when I saw Miss Etta James on stage. I was in shock that a woman was doing that, and now my granddaughter, Jasmine Johnson, got to see that. It was normal for her. I hope it showed her anything is possible.

The Gands are those rare folks who just give you space to do whatever you need to do, and I loved that. They asked me to help them at a fundraiser once, and I realized that people were not pulling out much cash. So, I got up on the stage and told them, "Let's all get out your wallets and put some money up in here. It's for charity, now. Come on." I did it in a nice, fun way, but I got the results.

During the Women's Blues Fest, I usually liked to go on at the middle of the show. It felt like the right place for me and I just loved playing with the audience. That's why I was there, to make sure they were having a good time. I called them out and had them participating. If there was a fine man out there, I sometimes put in a little extra effort. I loved that we were still preserving the history of the Blues, the nice clothes, and the interactive performances; it's important.

Things were tough on all of us since Daddy's passing. Patrick ended up homeless for a little while and bounced from one place to the next. By 2016, he was still out in Vegas with his girlfriend and his daughter, so he was trying to make things work.

I still didn't hear a lot from my daughter, but she was independent like that, and I had made peace with it. My father's side of the family had dealt with things in a different way. Some were trying to perform "tributes" and they were often the folks I never heard from again. The positive thing was that I had been able to reconnect with a lot of people, like the ones I grew up with and others who had lost touch along the way.

I had also rediscovered my mother's side of the family, thanks to people like Frager Thomas, who filled me in on what they have been up to. It turned out that they were very musical, as well, leaning more toward Gospel groups, but a couple were working with big names, such as Justin Timberlake. Knowing that I had music on both sides of my family made sense and gave me comfort that I followed the path I was destined to walk.

Marlvena Johnson was another lovely woman, who I ran into. She was from Greenwood, Mississippi, and her family grew up working on a plantation. She told me that once her mother said, "Guess who is at Mr. Pulley's house? It's your first cousin, B. B. King!" She said they all ran down that dirt road. She fell down, jumped back up, wiped off her knees, and kept running. She said Mr. King was sitting in a chair over by the corner. They asked if he would sing "Lucille," and he did. It was a memory for a lifetime. I heard lots of stories like that.

I still performed regularly at the Oak Street health centers and I had become sort of an unofficial spokesperson. They featured me on a few of their TV segments and commercials promoting the centers. I also talked them up everywhere I went and I even brought some of my famous friends to help entertain. It was almost comical to me that there I was singing and cutting up with older folk when I used to be out dancing every night in little tiny outfits, but they really enjoyed it.

I ran into so many people who related to my father and Blues music. They had a fondness for it, and it never failed to make them feel better. With my health troubles and the depression, it had been very healing for me to help others. I talked about how the center made me realize how important it was to take care of myself. They were doing things differently at that clinic because they were looking at senior care as more than just medicine. It was about a quality of life.

Dick moved on to another facility, actually a competitor called JenCare Senior Medical Centers owned by ChenMed, so I guess that concept was becoming popular. Maybe that meant ole Shirley needed to travel around to meet all of these seniors!

One person who I haven't mentioned yet is Gerald Noel, my partner and companion for over eleven years. A well-respected saxophone player, he opened for my father many times as part of the Bobby Bland Band. They played hundreds of shows together, and my father had great respect for Gerald. I met him around 2006 at one of their gigs and we just hit it off. I instantly felt comfortable with him, partly because I knew Daddy thought highly of him and having Daddy's stamp of approval meant a lot to me.

He said that Daddy often told him to ". . . do the best you can when you perform and always be professional." Gerald also toured with Junior Walker and the All-Stars, so I liked that he had been able to make a name for himself and kept working in this tough industry.

After we became involved, I asked him to join me at some of my shows as part of the band. He was very helpful in managing the other musicians and keeping the band tight. He'd seen a lot of change in this business as one of the true remaining musicians dedicated to playing Classical Jazz, R&B, and some Blues as a way of keeping that kind of music alive for another generation. He said to me, "Lawyers practice law, doctors practice medicine, and musicians should practice their craft, the music." He'd never liked the trend of folks playing to recorded tracks and using technology to reproduce the beautiful sounds of a live band.

Another thing I'd come to realize was that he stood by me through some tough times. He was with my after my cancer diagnosis and the treatments. He helped me every time I had an appointment and watched over me to make sure I was taking care of my health. When Daddy was touring, we went backstage to see him, and he told Gerald, "Thank you for taking care of my daughter."

When I was called onstage at Buddy Guy's place that night, Gerald was there, too. He told everyone, "There are four musical giants on that stage: B.B. King, Buddy Guy, George Benson, and Shirley King." He told me that he was proud when Daddy called me onstage. "At that moment, he was passing the baton on to you. Sometimes, the baton can be passed on and we fail to realize it. It was passed to you, and now everyone is watching to see what you will say and do."

He was right about that. They were watching, and that was especially true when we found out that Daddy had passed. Gerald was by my side as I dealt with the news and even when the local TV stations came to the house for an interview. He helped me deal with the difficulty of losing someone who was so important in my life. He recognized that I had a spiritual connection with my father and that I felt his power and strength through the sunshine. Not everyone understood that, but he did.

It was also important to me that Gerald fell in love with music early on. When he was growing up in Baton Rouge, he was in a music program led by the Superintendent of Music, a man named Harry Evans, who was the brother of Bill Evans, a world-famous Jazz pianist. So, he was exposed to music and the arts in elementary school and that helped him develop a real love for music, which is something we don't see as much today. Gerald said, "We can love many things, but are we passionate about the things that we love?"

That was one of the reasons I put so much energy into my Blues in the Schools program. Exposing children to music (and especially the Blues) at a young age helped to grow that appreciation and plant the seed for a new generation. When I shared my stories and songs with children, I got such a welcome reception and they were truly excited by a type of music that they had never heard before. It was very important to me that I do my part to help motivate a new generation of people to appreciate the Blues.

What I'd come to realize was that maybe my father did leave me something very valuable by giving his blessing to Gerald. He knew that no matter what happened to him, Gerald would be looking after his daughter. Our relationship has not been easy by any means, but we have survived. He stood by me during those tough times and I think Daddy would be happy knowing that we are still together.

It was also helpful to have someone who truly believed in me and my talent. He always said that there are many other entertainers out there—Mary J. Blige, Lady Gaga, Britney Spears, Alicia Keys—so many talented performers, but not like me. He told me, "You have the talent, the voice, and a world-renowned name. You have it all. A lot of entertainers wish they had what you have."

My overseas performances were still in demand, and I regularly went to Brazil, Portugal, and Germany to sing at festivals and other events. It was still exciting and inspiring to see so many people from different parts of the world who loved the Blues. I always made sure to salute my father and do something in his honor. I felt like it was my job to carry on the tradition as best I could. I couldn't be him, but I could help keep his name alive.

Things were still being worked out with my father's estate, and I tried not to get too involved in that, because it got real messy. It was disappointing that I hadn't gotten anything to remember him by, but I tried to focus on the positives and keep him alive through my music.

I took my show on the road and performed in a lot of places where Daddy used to play. I also promoted the Blues in the Schools initiative, which was a way to keep Blues music alive for the next generation. That meant going to schools and having talks and maybe performing a little bit to keep that interest going. I also worked on an album of new music. I got my website going and I felt positive about the future. I decided that I needed to keep focused on what I did best and that was not only good for me, but my hope was that it would keep my father's legacy alive.

Memories of my father still came back to me at the most un-likely times. I heard a word or phrase and it unlocked another feeling or memory of him. People might think it was strange, but I heard his voice talk to me. I remember the way he always called me "pretty girl" and made me feel so loved. I learned that it was important to honor and remember him, and also to live for myself.

Someone told me that my father wasn't like a star; he was more like a moon. When I asked why, he said it was because a star burns out, but a moon never does.

EPILOGUE

Doing tributes to my father always seemed to bring about good things. When I did that Memphis tribute that I talked about at the beginning of this book, it was a real tough time for me. It was my dad's first birthday since he had passed and it was real hard. Not only that, I was having a lot of other issues. Life was just getting in the way. I think I hadn't fully processed the fact that the most important man in my life was gone forever. I guess I didn't want to face that reality.

That guy who was at the club in Nashville with me, where I was drinking the Blues Juice, the one whose name I couldn't remember, was the man who would be my co-writer. He was the one who would help me on this journey to tell my story. This project, with the help of Phil and Lara Stark, brought me out of the negativity that had surrounded my father. The court case and fight over his estate was still going on, that's for sure, but I felt like I had been given a second chance, a new lease on life.

This was now my time to show what I could do and how I was going to have my own name while still honoring my dad. I moved from "B. B. King's daughter, Shirley King" to "Shirley King, Daughter of the Blues, and daughter of the great legend, B. B. King."

I had to move on and keep the music alive. It was the only thing I knew how to do and I felt it was the reason I was put on this earth. I was able to bring people joy, to help them turn a tear into a smile, and that was a privilege I didn't take lightly. I came to realize that no matter what happened in the past or what my future held, the one constant was performing.

After all, it was in my blood.

CPSIA information can be obtained
at www.ICGtesting.com
Printed in the USA
BVHW040759220419
546163BV00014B/105/P